CONNECTIONS

Actionable Guidance on Solo Practice and Small Law Firm Business Development

MERANDA M. VIEYRA

AMERICAN BAR ASSOCIATION
Law Practice Division

Cover design by Elizabeth Kulak/ABA Design

Printed in the United States of America.

29 28 27 26 25 5 4 3 2 1

Library of Congress Cataloging-in-Publication Data
Names: Vieyra, Meranda M., author.
Title: Connections : actionable guidance on solo practice and small law firm business development / Meranda M. Vieyra.
Description: Chicago : American Bar Association, 2025. | Includes bibliographical references. | Summary: "This is a guide, a "how to" book for helping solo and small law firm lawyers learn how to start or do more business development through in-person and digital activities. The book is broken down into themed chapters so you can self-diagnose issues that plague your business development"-- Provided by publisher.
Identifiers: LCCN 2025026534 (print) | LCCN 2025026535 (ebook) | ISBN 9781639056378 (paperback) | ISBN 9781639056385 (epub)
Subjects: LCSH: Law firms--United States. | Solo law practice--United States. | Small business--Law and legislation--United States. | Law offices--United States.
Classification: LCC KF318 .V57 2025 (print) | LCC KF318 (ebook) | DDC 340.068--dc23/eng/20250603
LC record available at https://lccn.loc.gov/2025026534
LC ebook record available at https://lccn.loc.gov/2025026535

Discounts are available for books ordered in bulk. Special consideration is given to state bars, CLE programs, and other bar-related organizations. Inquire at Book Publishing, ABA Publishing, American Bar Association, 321 N. Clark Street, Chicago, Illinois 60654–7598.

www.shopABA.org

For Gordon, Itzel, and Nelle

Contents

Preface

True story. I met a great business attorney a few years back when she was an associate at a medium-sized law firm in Denver. She was not a major stakeholder in the firm, and she wasn't a rainmaker. Rather, she was a new mom and young professional trying to carve out time for personal and professional obligations. She was like me, juggling work in the legal industry with the pressures of being a working mother. My interest in helping her was genuine. In addition to our mutual experience working in law, we shared a common interest in parenting, which we both came at with humor and honesty. We had a connection.

I moved on from working with her law firm, and we chose to stay in contact—we kept the connection. Fast forward to the beginning of the pandemic when she reached out needing advice because she wanted to go solo. She was now a brand-new business owner with a laundry list of questions regarding marketing her new solo law firm. I was happy to hear that she was taking the leap into entrepreneurship, and I openly gave her the guidance she needed without asking for payment. To be frank, chances were that she didn't have it, and I didn't desperately need it, so money was never exchanged. After her law firm opened, again we kept the connection going. We stayed in contact over the years, with visibility in each other's circles limited to digital touchpoints through my email campaign and LinkedIn.

That same lawyer, who was a member of the ABA, connected me with her colleague who was looking for someone to write an article for an ABA publication. I jumped at the opportunity, and I wrote the article. After all, the article's proposed subject matter was exactly in my niche—solo and small law firm marketing and business development. My dedication to service in the solo and small business world pointed directly back to my passion for entrepreneurship and supporting the small businesses of the legal industry—law firms with ten attorneys or less. My article was then passed on to someone who was looking for an author for a business development book for solo and small law firms to be published by the ABA.

And that's that. Through a series of intentional activities, I received a book contract that led to the text you are reading right now. How this professional opportunity to write a book for the ABA worked for me is how it works for everyone —through ***Connections***.

Introduction

Connections is your guide, a "how-to" book for helping solo and small law firm lawyers learn how to start or do more business development through in-person and digital activities. Business development is a wide topic in the legal industry. The material we cover will be limited to the following scope through the lens of solo or small law firms:

- An explanation of the processes and systems needed to identify business development opportunities, sources, and leads for lawyers in B2B and B2C practice areas.[1]
- High-level insight and tips into the business development skills most attorneys in B2B and B2C practice areas need to develop, including communication, branding, project management, and personal marketing.

I have broken *Connections* down into themed chapters so you can self-diagnose issues that plague your business development.

[1] B2B practice areas, meaning "Business to Business," are practice areas where the lawyer works with corporations, businesspeople, and others involved in business transactions or business settings. Examples of B2B practice areas aside from general corporate law are mergers & acquisitions, corporate immigration, intellectual property, business succession planning, securities law, and even white-collar law, depending on the situation.

This is contrasted by B2C, or "Business to Consumer," practice areas, where the lawyer works directly with individuals and families. Lawyers who work in B2C areas include family law, criminal defense, DUI defense, trusts & estates, as well as plaintiff personal injury and other civil litigation.

Although they are self-contained, the chapters can also be read and followed one by one in order through the end as a roadmap to guide you through the major tenets of a personalized business development strategy with the tactical activities and KPIs[2] needed to track success.

It's crucial to note that the responsibility of reviewing and understanding ethical rules in marketing and business development activities lies with lawyers and law firms. These rules, which vary from state to state, must be thoroughly reviewed in all jurisdictions where they practice. This includes, but is not limited to, regulations related to advertising, solicitation, and communication about the lawyer or law firm's services. It's only after this comprehensive review that a business development strategy or a new marketing campaign can be developed. The business development insights in this book are provided from a general perspective and do not replace the need to adhere to specific state ethical rules and requirements.

Connections includes special areas or features in each chapter titled "Good Thinking" and "Spotlights." The intention behind these vignettes matters because they add deeper details and professional development to the book. Having an open mind when absorbing these areas will lead to inspiration, a-ha moments, and ideas regarding the professional development needed to create the law practice you want.

The Good Thinking sections, scattered throughout most chapters, are valuable to your business development planning process. They provide a fun read and a boost of knowledge on specific marketing and business development aspects discussed in the chapter. Think of these snippets as a casual yet informative chat, offering sage advice and interesting data on small law firm business development. Through the Good Thinking sections, you'll feel more informed and knowledgeable regarding a variety of common issues that attorneys face.

---

[2] A KPI is a key performance indicator, a measurable metric for quantifying your law firm's business development and marketing successes. KPIs for law firms can vary, but examples can include return on investment, client acquisition numbers, or even revenue received from sales of legal services.

The Spotlights in *Connections* are not just for reading but for action. These snippets provide direct business development pathways and examples alternating between business-based (B2B) and consumer-based law practices (B2C). These insights come from years of hands-on experience in business development projects with solo and small law firms. The Spotlights are interactive; they contain advice that can be used to learn something new, try something different, or avoid an expensive business development mistake. When it comes to the Spotlights included in this book, look for similarities between your law practice or goals and the examples. Even if the Spotlight isn't a perfect description or match of what you are looking for in your career, don't discard it. Instead, look for commonalities, such as the similarities between audience, goals, and results, which make the Spotlights easy to learn from for various law practices for various purposes. Their adaptability means they can be tailored to your specific needs by you, your staff, or your marketing team.

Though *Connections* will be in printed form, additional materials are available on the Denver Legal Marketing website (www.denverlegalmarketing.com) to help solo and small law firm practitioners create or update their law firms' business development plans.

1

Centers

> ***The key to competing and surviving against Wal-Mart is to focus your business into a niche or pocket where you can leverage your strengths in the local marketplace.***
>
> **—Michael Bergdahl**

This chapter focuses on how lawyers become centers of influence through practice area focus and niche. Business development can be made easier for small law firms when they have less competition in larger practice areas and/or specialize in certain demographics or legal issues. Essentially, when the pool is smaller, you are bigger. This chapter supports solo and small firm attorneys interested in developing a focus for their law practice based on a specific legal issue or client. A niche law practice can change the economics of your law firm and build more loyalty and expertise for your practice.

***

You have met the lawyer with the enviable niche practice. They have rock star status in the legal community. Everyone knows who they are and what they do. They speak at high-influence conferences, are the go-to for legal commentary in the press, and collect coveted awards in their practice areas. Some of them have a velvet rope in their practice, with access to their time so limited that they have an eager line of new clients waiting in queue. These attorneys are go-to problem-solvers in their communities and are easily recognizable by their reputations and services. Niche practice attorneys seem to be everywhere when it comes to their pockets of expertise, and because they are "the one," they get to charge for it. Focused legal services provide subject matter expertise that, depending on the issue or the audience, can allow for higher rates. Pulling it together, a niche isn't just a tool for small law firm practitioners; it is a power tool.

Niche is defined as:

> [a] niche market is the subset of the market on which a specific product is focused. The market niche defines the product features aimed at satisfying specific market needs, as well as the price range, production quality and the demographics that it is intended to target. It is also a small market segment. Sometimes, a product or service can be entirely designed to satisfy a niche market.[1]

Put more simply, a niche law practice is a focused law practice (or even a small aspect of your larger law practice that is focused), and you can absolutely create one.

DO YOU NEED A LAW PRACTICE NICHE?

It is impossible to be everything to everyone. Working in a smaller law firm without a determined focus within your broader legal practice or general practice areas can make your professional life feel like you are constantly drinking from a fire hose. Finding a focus for your legal work is a great way to create and maintain a notable reputation that feeds your business development strategy and gives you more control over your results than you would otherwise have. Attorneys can

[1] https://en.wikipedia.org/wiki/Niche_market.

stumble backward into a focus for their law practice, they can deliberately seek a focus out, or sometimes they fall into a blend of the two.

A few of the perks of having a niche law practice:

- Helps you say "yes and no" to clients and opportunities.
- Allows you to charge more in your specialty.
- Aids you in creating a consistent presence in the legal communities and other professional communities you are involved in.

Specialized legal services up the game in business development for B2B and B2C practice areas. When you are immersed in a specific community or certain legal issue, it is common to seek out knowledge on the subject matter through the consumption of articles, podcasts, and books to keep abreast of industry changes—because you are genuinely interested. When you arrive at an industry event, the pressure for sales is off, and you have plenty to discuss even casually. Business development and networking conversations run smoothly because you are simply "talking" about something you care about and know well.

This level of focus on a subject matter, a legal issue, or an industry develops your knowledge base, which makes you more confident in your interactions and the legal services you provide. You won't be looking for something to share at a networking happy hour because you arrived at the event already informed and armed with thoughtful questions to ask. You won't be an outsider at industry events, because you are understanding and empathetic to the challenges of the people you are trying to do business with. Business development activities, such as networking conversations, aren't so grueling because when you are concentrated on a certain subject, law, population, or legal topic, you are ready to distinctively add high-level insight to conversations related to your niche.

Your specialized knowledge is not just impressive; it's essential. It sets you apart when meeting new contacts and instills confidence in your unique services. Your skills are finely tuned in your niche. You'll find that decision-making for your clients is a whole different process because of your deep industry understanding. Being strategic for your clients becomes second nature as you understand their challenges and what to avoid. Your niche expertise makes you more knowledgeable and effective, translating to superior client representation in a defined area.

Even when a particular issue in your niche doesn't pique your curiosity, the necessity of staying abreast of the latest news, trends, and updates is a continuous form of professional development. It augments your ability to readily help others through your legal services. This ongoing awareness directly contributes to your business development. Maintaining this "in the know" status is an advantage that others may not have, simply because they haven't put in the effort.

A lawyer specializing in the restaurant and hospitality industry is not just a legal advisor to their community but also a trusted source for information. They should be well-versed in the laws and regulations that apply to restaurants and understand the current issues and long-standing problems affecting the industry. This comprehensive knowledge base gives them a competitive edge over other lawyers and law firms with similar offerings and builds trust with their clients.

B2B SPOTLIGHT: FOCUSED PRACTICE IN AGRIBUSINESS

An agricultural lawyer focuses their law practice on the needs of a rural community in Wyoming to provide business legal services specifically to farmers and ranchers. Smaller populations sometimes shun outsiders, so trust in the lawyer has to be earned. Upon moving to Wyoming to hang their shingle, the attorney understood that they would need to live and work in the community where they intended to practice law. They met with a few city leaders before signing a commercial real estate lease. These city leaders gave insight into the importance of reputation and visibility in their community. This small town had a strong word-of-mouth culture, as it was sparsely populated with lots of distance between neighbors. The law firm's location in the city center, where everyone was bound to see it at some point when they drove into town to pick up supplies and mail, was a wise choice for business development and marketing.

The lawyer's brand also had to reflect the community's values. The attorney was a quick study, incorporating long-standing and general rural values such as privacy and cooperation into their law firm. They added text related to the law firm's corporate values to the website and all promotional materials to confirm its alignment with these traditional views. Special attention was paid to the marketing imagery selected to resonate with the farming and ranching community. Additionally, they understood this community didn't want to be observed or disturbed. So, they knew that previous client testimonials and case studies would be hard to incorporate into their marketing.

To support their niche, the attorney consistently sought education and information through CLEs, publications, and professional organizations related to agribusiness. They stayed updated on the state and federal laws that specifically apply to agricultural businesses, including mandates from regulatory agencies. This consistent education allowed them to draft concise updates for their clients on the new laws, backed up with practical advice on why they matter to their clients, businesses, and the future.

Operating as a small-town lawyer requires careful business development. The pool of potential clients is as precise as it is small, and the law firm's service offerings, tailored to the ranching and farming business, further narrow their business development opportunities. The attorney, however, is committed to earning the community's trust. They attend community events sincerely aiming to connect with new and existing clients and referral sources. They've learned from other community members that the annual projects completed by the local 4-H youth organization are

(Continued)

B2B SPOTLIGHT: FOCUSED PRACTICE IN AGRIBUSINESS *(CONTINUED)*

an excellent way to get to know everyone, so they make sure to attend. They complement this with financial sponsorship of 4-H events, reinforcing the law firm's branding that the community is already familiar with due to the town center location of the law practice.

The rural values this attorney shares with the community are also seen in the thought leadership they publish in the local newspaper, offering proactive insights into the most common issues plaguing the ranching and farming business owners. This includes employment issues, updating and maintaining partnership contracts, navigation of regulatory compliance, and diffusing disputes. The local newspaper has a strong following, so the articles validate the brand and the lawyer's law practice offerings. At the same time, these articles build their reputation in the community, enhance their CV with agribusiness-related publications, and develop trust with the intended audience by generously giving expertise and knowledge on the legal issues that keep them up at night.

This B2B example shows that niche law practices can work even in a small community with a limited number of potential clients. The attorney researched their audience to understand what was important to them and then made business decisions to connect strategically. Looking carefully at their law practice decisions, big and small, we see a lesson in building trust and its importance in a niche. The potential clients of this law firm were wary of outsiders, so trust is built slowly through careful consideration of the firm's brand and values, building location, community sponsorship, and even the type of curated thought leadership they place in the local newspaper.

Choosing a niche can be a strategic business decision by a lawyer or law firm at any point in their business life cycle. It's a decision that can bring unique value to a practice, especially when it aligns with issues or populations that are already of interest. A niche can also be uncovered while deeply committing to a particular case. Common niches include industry focuses, legal issue specialty, or even a niche population such as Spanish speakers. For example, a lawyer might leverage their fluency in Spanish to specialize in immigration law, particularly with Venezuelan and other Spanish-speaking asylum seekers. This intentional niche in immigration law capitalizes on their language and legal skills while being a strategic business decision.

On the other hand, attorneys can also develop a niche unintentionally in their law practice, showcasing their adaptability and open-mindedness. Perhaps their subject matter expertise was revealed during a key client engagement or when they took on an issue that many of their clients face, such as a civil rights practice that ends up focusing on plaintiff police brutality matters. Another example would be civil litigators who work on a precedent-setting case that feeds their trial practice for the rest of their careers. This is also seen in attorneys representing one professional athlete and being so good at it that they become "the lawyer" whom sports professionals, including players, managers, and owners, call for criminal defense. It works both ways—a niche can be developed on purpose or stumbled upon unintentionally.

Niche practices serve a specific purpose. They might focus on the physical location of their clients, such as a particular city, or on a specific client profile, such as pet owners. For instance, a civil attorney with a general practice could shift their focus to animal rights, handling cases related to defending dog bites, pet custody matters, and service animals. The purpose of a niche is to concentrate on how your legal services can best serve a specific part of the population in a particular way.

With a niche, you know what you are seeking when it comes to business development. This makes promotional activities easier as you know where to go and what to say. You get to choose your clients and determine whether the fit is right rather than the other way around. Deciding to pursue a niche does not mean you must turn down all other work that comes your way. Instead, a niche reflects your specialized abilities. You can do the more general work, the less specialized representations, and so on. However, in your niche, you serve clients differently—and better.

HOW TO DEVELOP YOUR LAW PRACTICE NICHE

If you are in a niche practice, you should aim to be a subject matter expert on your audience, which includes knowledge of their demographics, issues, challenges, and so on. The client experience in a niche practice should feel more customized than in a general law practice. The goals of your practice should be accounted for along with a clear understanding of what the market looks like, including your legal industry competition. Finally, the pain points that your target audience experiences should be addressed through your marketing and, if possible, through your legal services. Developing a focused practice helps you become a center of influence in your community. So, the goals associated with a focused law practice should be broken down into big buckets.

#1: Begin with Your End in Mind

Ultimately, pursuing a niche is up to you. If you are trying to develop a more focused practice, the question you are trying to answer here is related to your preferences in your professional career and what type of practice you want long term. You must know your end goal to compare your potential niche against it. This will aid in determining the viability of a niche for you, your practice, and your location.

Look at your work for the past few years to find a niche. Do you notice any trends or similarities between engagements? Are there certain types of clients that you enjoy working with more or get along with better? Maybe you have social, economic, and political issues that you have always wanted to pursue in your legal career—how can you do more with them? Do your clients do business in a focused industry or certain area, or are there other commonalities, such as revenue or size? Do your clients all have the same legal issue (for example, criminal defense in DUI cases or corporate defense in work-related injury cases)? Attorneys can easily fall into a niche practice based on the market's demands, the needs of a specific client group, or the lawyer's abilities. Looking at patterns in your client engagements can expose a niche focus for you. You then develop your business development strategy by reverse engineering the goal.

B2C SPOTLIGHT: NICHE PRACTICE IN FAMILY LAW

A family law attorney wants to develop a niche in their established solo law firm practice. The attorney first looks for patterns in their engagements, and they note that most of their clients are Spanish speaking and live within a 20-mile radius of their law office. This family lawyer also finds that the clients primarily seek representation with post-decree custody issues. In this example, the attorney's niche could revolve around the custody-related problems that Spanish-speaking parents face in their city or county.

In this example, they will use this demographic focus to learn more about this segment of the Spanish-speaking population, including deeper data points that indicate other commonalities that correlate with location, such as income and education level. They can also review online information, local community forums, and social media groups to start a list of bilingual business providers in their area that service the same population. The attorney will then use this information to create a niche for their practice backed by a targeted business development campaign connected to marketing

(Continued)

B2C SPOTLIGHT: NICHE PRACTICE IN FAMILY LAW *(CONTINUED)*

channels. The attorney will begin networking with family therapists and other lawyers in the area to begin the process of being on their shortlists for client referrals.

The attorney, in a proactive move, prepares a series of recorded webinars. These webinars, presented in Spanish, provide insightful information on how the state courts view post-decree custody-related issues, frequently asked questions about the family law legal process, and strategies to protect one's interests in an active case. This proactive approach not only demonstrates the attorney's commitment to their clients but also ensures that potential clients are well informed about the legal process. These pre-recorded messages live on the attorney's website, making them easily shareable with their referral sources and any website traffic. The website's analytics tools provide detailed information about who views the videos, how long they watch, and what actions they take next, making the videos' impact entirely trackable. The videos end with text on-screen that confirms the law firm's contact information with a call to action to connect with the family law attorney to learn more. These webinars are distributed through business partners that serve the same population as part of a marketing funnel driving interest in the firm.

#2: Determine Your Market

Especially if your niche feels common or crowded, be sure to do some market research for yourself. In the B2C example, the family attorney looking to reach Spanish-speaking clients might need to know the statistics regarding divorces in their community. Statistics regarding gender and age can help with messaging or help determine which social media platforms will reach the audience best. The American Bar Association suggested "[s]ixty-six percent of lawyers who use social media personally for professional purposes use it for career development and networking, including 48% of solos, 63% of lawyers in firms of 2–9 lawyers . . . [and] *[o]ther uses for social media for professional purposes include client development (51%), education and awareness (49%),* community engagement (43%), and case investigation (21%)."[2] Many attorneys forget that the business side of social media platforms is a research tool that can be used to learn more about your community.

Understanding your market helps you identify your target audience, determine how to reach them in person and online, and determine what they need to hear about the legal issue you want to resolve. In B2C practice areas, market research through social media might include a study of any of the following:

- Age and gender
- Income, education, and occupation
- Family structure and family diversity
- Religion and sexual orientation

Especially in consumer-based practices, social media research can help shape your strategy and your messaging.

For business attorneys looking to learn more about their audiences, social media provides insight into demographics and firmographics. Firmographics is defined as "sets of characteristics to segment prospect organizations. What demographics are to people, firmographics are to organizations."[3] This snapshot of information provides you with insight into their geography, structure, financial status, and financial performance. These can be key metrics in determining whether a niche will be profitable and sustainable in a niche law practice.

---

[2] https://www.americanbar.org/groups/law_practice/resources/legal-technology-resource-center/tech-survey/2020/ (emphasis added).

[3] https://en.wikipedia.org/wiki/Firmographics.

GOOD THINKING

Regardless of how good you are at what you do, you have competition. At any moment, over a million lawyers are practicing law in the United States. One ABA survey reported that the number of active lawyers as of January 2024 was 1,322,649.[4] Don't let competition scare you. If you know where the competition lies for your solo or small law firm, you can continue to innovate and develop your law firm's unique brand while keeping the quality of your legal services and customer experience high. Let the competition motivate you.

#3: Get to Know Your Market

Other lawyers will do similar work in similar spaces, even within a niche. When developing your niche, be sure to know your competition and what they are doing as it relates to your focus. Savvy attorneys look, even if a cursory glance, at the marketing of existing firms that could be viewed as competition. When reviewing your competitor's information, pay attention to their messaging as much as you note their look and feel. This information provides insight into how *they* are talking to *your* ideal client.

Saturation is an additional area to consider in a niche market. It will be challenging (but not impossible) for you to generate revenue for your law practice if there are too many attorneys and options to choose from. Saturation can be apparent, especially when you can see the volume of personal injury billboards lining both sides of the major streets in your city. An overpopulated legal market doesn't necessarily mean that you can't compete. But it will mean that your practice must somehow be distinct from the competition. For example, suppose everyone in the personal injury space has similar credentials and price points regarding fee collection and comparable

[4] https://www.abalegalprofile.com/demographics.html#:~:text=There%20are%20more%20than%201.3,every%20U.S.%20state%20and%20territory.

results. In that case, your personal injury practice must stand out somehow, maybe through multilingual attorneys, 24/7 access to legal advice, and so on. Saturated markets can still be profitable if you can find a way to win the battle for attention and stand out.

An additional area of market research worth mentioning is your niche's narrowness. It is possible to have your niche market be too small to generate revenue to sustain a practice. A niche that is too narrow could leave your law firm sensitive to market changes or even in a drought in the pool of potential clients. A niche that is too small will have clear indicators, such as difficulty in finding clients or lack of engagement with the content your law firm is producing. If you are nervous that your niche is too small, you can expand your focus to include other demographics or legal issues. Remind yourself that you can always expand or contract your niche if the demand changes.

#4: Know Your Audience

Attorneys who have a niche practice know the challenges of the population they serve and how their legal services help. They also know what the benefits of their legal services are and how they connect emotionally to their target audience, maybe by touching on hopes or specific outcomes. Understanding what makes your client tick is a great byproduct of the research done to initially determine a niche. This effort doesn't cost a lot of money, as you can learn a lot through a review of social media profiles regarding demographics and preferences. You can also gather your own information through a custom survey or poll.

You will want to take note of the legal services needs of your audience that are currently unmet or underserved. For instance, a trusts and estates attorney might log into their law firm's Facebook business account to access the business suite. Their law practice services a densely populated suburban community with lots of families. In reviewing the demographic information provided through the Facebook business suite, they learn that much of their target market are parents to college freshmen. In response to that information, the attorney might adjust their marketing to provide information and insight into the legal forms that the parents of young adults need to consider after their child turns 18 years old. This might include blog posts and social media messaging on the healthcare proxy and power of attorney forms. Remember, matching up your niche legal services to the needs of your niche audience is the goal.

Developing your niche will develop your law practice simultaneously. As your understanding of the community you serve grows, so will your empathy. This ability to relate builds trust, allowing your small law practice services to compete with larger law firms and win. These efforts to develop a niche also help you learn about the world of your ideal audience and fine-tune your brand and your marketing so that you can speak directly to the ideal client. It will identify new opportunities for you to help your customer base. In the B2C situation we visited previously, the attorney might find that clients circle back to them for referrals to other Spanish-speaking attorneys, such as criminal defense or trusts and estates. This opens another aspect of business development for the firm through reciprocated referrals from other attorneys who serve the same population. A niche law practice coupled with a strategy aimed at long-term presence and establishment of authority can make you the top lawyer locally, nationally, and even internationally.

B2B SPOTLIGHT: SPECIALIZED PRACTICE IN BUSINESS LAW

A business attorney enters their legal practice with a broad intention to work in corporate law and transactions. Law is their second career, as they left a previous life in banking and finance. This attorney reviews their previous corporate client matters to determine if there are any patterns that lead to a niche offering. Their research involves looking at types of businesses, industries, size of businesses, locations, and revenue generated. From this review of past engagements, they determine that they find the most joy and the most personal engagement in supporting the legal needs of small businesses. The attorney decides to silo their corporate law practice by working specifically in a niche with start-ups and entrepreneurs.

Here is another example of how a niche can help develop a business development and marketing funnel in a law practice. If this B2B attorney wants to service the new business owner community, they will need to learn more about them. They might discover that a large majority of new businesses register with a certain professional organization in their community, such as a Better Business Bureau, for help with initial start-up issues. If the attorney then formed a complementary business relationship with that professional organization, even through a paid membership, they could provide proactive information on the legal side of entrepreneurship. This might take the form of monthly contributions to their email newsletter authored by the lawyer that provide forward-thinking information with a clear call to action to drive interest back to the firm.

In the B2B example, understanding the challenges of their customer base might lead them to develop more business relationships with local CPA firms, marketing firms, and the like to refer trusted professionals to their small business clients. They can also develop a reciprocal relationship with intellectual property lawyers in a law firm of a similar size. The attorney could repurpose the thought leadership they are producing for the Better Business Bureau's email newsletter by asking their business partners, such as the CPA firms, to reshare those articles in their own newsletters or social media channels, broadening the reach of the business attorney's promotional efforts. The attorney's articles are also validated in the business community by being originally published in a Better Business

Bureau publication. The niche offerings allow the lawyer to really focus on the exact issues and business partners needed to reach the target community of potential clients.

INCLUDING INCLUSION

Modern, small law practices include aspects of diversity, equity, and inclusion (DEI) in their business development. Broadening your networking and business development by intentionally including people who are different from you is just smart. Diversity doesn't have one silo and is shown in your professional network in different ways. One of the most obvious is cultural diversity, but when you widen the lens, you see that a thriving professional network includes different backgrounds, industries, and even professional roles. This adds diversity in perspective and mindsets around your law practice, which can be helpful in solo and small law firms, where the variety of colleagues is limited.

Adding a DEI component to your business development strategy for a niche practice will broaden your horizons while challenging your assumptions. This growth isn't available just to small law firm lawyers; this growth happens for everyone when they are exposed to new ideas and insights. This widened social intelligence regarding people who are different from you and your own community adds depth to your business development at the same time as it adds an edge.

Across the board, DEI contributes to the health and success of law practices as businesses and professional service providers. Having a DEI component in your niche business development strategy can only strengthen your efforts and improve your law practice. There are a variety of ways to add the inclusion of others who are not like you to your professional networking and business development. Lawyers looking to go down this path will want to add a few prompts to augment their research related to their law practice niche to include DEI.

Questions to ask:

- *Who is missing from the table or the larger conversations related to your niche?* It is helpful to check for blind spots when developing a niche practice. Determining who is being served by your law practice is not enough—who also needs these services but isn't being currently served is a good question, too. In the example of the B2B lawyer who wants to focus on start-ups and entrepreneurs, they might notice a trend as it relates to women-owned or veteran-owned start-ups falling behind where other start-ups with less diversity in ownership are thriving. They might consider how they can serve this underserved population through legal services, networking, connections, or even education. What's helpful is that in marketing and business development everything doesn't have to be done all at once. Having a few resources on your website related to a diverse population within your niche and their legal issues (that you help with) can be a good start.

- *How diverse is your law firm's team?* In the example of the B2C solo law firm connecting with Spanish-speaking family law clients, it would be helpful if the law firm's staff exhibited diversity in culture by being bilingual in Spanish. This prompt touches a bit on recruiting and staffing, but it is important to consider. Operational issues like staffing bleed into marketing and business development efforts for any law firm, regardless of size. Returning to the B2C practice, the lawyer could start the niche based on their own fluency in a second language and can deepen the offering through the intentional bilingual staffing of their cases.
- *How can you show DEI in your business development and marketing?* Showing DEI in your niche practice isn't much of an obstacle, even when you have limited resources. It just takes intention. An easy example of how to add DEI in business development and networking would be joining a DEI-related committee within a larger organization in which you are already a member. Maybe you are a member of the chamber of commerce in your city. Review their offerings, as many have existing DEI efforts through committees, events, causes, and so on that you can easily be a part of.

GOOD THINKING

There are many options when it comes to promoting your law practice. "The leading channels for marketing across all firm sizes in 2020 were event sponsorship (48%), LinkedIn (42%), email (41%), Facebook (33%), and print (21%)."[5] *For a solo or small law firm lawyer looking to do more promotion, it will feel like choice overload. But remember that you don't have to engage with every marketing and promotional opportunity out there. These decisions are made easier when you start with your target audience to determine what methods of communication they use. Is it mostly email and Facebook? Or maybe they get their information from a certain professional publication and LinkedIn? You can then determine how you can engage with those platforms in a way that respects your brand, budget, and time constraints.*

Participation in DEI committees is a wonderful item to add to your website biography and can lead to more informed and interesting blog posts on your firm's website. An additional proactive idea on how to show DEI in your niche marketing is to review the demographics of your target audience and adjust where you need to so you can connect with your audience better. For example, if you have stock images on your website, do they include photos of diverse people? If you work with a multinational audience, is your website translated into different languages?

- *How will you keep your DEI efforts updated?* Consider how you are staying informed as it relates to not only your niche but any sub-niches in diverse populations that you have identified. Technology can help a small law firm lawyer stay current through targeted Google Alerts, intentional choice in media they are consuming, and the organizations they are a part of.

---

[5] https://www.americanbar.org/groups/law_practice/resources/legal-technology-resource-center/tech-survey/2020/.

> For example, joining a diverse chamber of commerce helps a business lawyer looking to meet professionals and include diversity in their networking. They are also able to attend the events and educational programming put on by the diverse chamber of commerce, which will help them grow as a person and a professional.

Adding a DEI component or considerations to your business development plan is easy and smart. This is a blind spot for many solo practitioners and small law firms, leading them to be passed over for success and growth opportunities that come from adding diverse perspectives and populations into their law practice.

Oftentimes, the fruit is hanging lower than they realize. For example, maybe your family law newsletter is in English, but you can have it translated into multiple languages through a cost-effective online service, increasing its audience and efficacy. Or is it possible that your business law firm works with entrepreneurs but, as a women-owned law firm, develops a real passion for working with women-owned start-ups in the tech space? By digging into your niche and using an inclusive lens, you find many different types of clients and communities for your law firm.

CENTER OF INFLUENCE

Being a center of influence in a community through an identifiable niche will blow up your network—in a good way. Focusing on who you are reaching and what you are saying to them will improve your business development, leading to better potential clients and networking prospects. Once you have established yourself as a center of influence in a focused area, the opportunities for business development can feel vast.

Having a niche practice allows you to dive deeper into the professions that are adjacent to your practice to become well-known or visible in their circles. In the B2C example of Spanish-speaking clients in the family law practice area, word-of-mouth referrals can spread like wildfire. Spanish-speaking people usually hang around with other Spanish-speaking people, and they share recommendations about good service providers, like lawyers. In this scenario, the Spanish-language family law practice starts by networking with bilingual family therapists, but they continue to expand their network to include other Spanish-speaking professionals such as mortgage providers, real estate agents, and bankers.

A niche gives you trust-based networking, which sets a strong foundation for your law practice and cements your business development relationships. A human-to-human connection with your audience is important in both B2B and B2C law practices. The understanding that comes with empathy can be channeled toward meaningful action through your legal services. You will learn more about your audience through networking with others in the field. So when the opportunity arises to meet referral sources to your practice that serve the same type of client or are in the same niche as you—jump on them.

GOOD THINKING

Social capital is a term that attorneys in networking mode need to be familiar with. Social capital has many definitions but, in this context, it can be defined as "a set of shared values or resources that allows individuals to work together in a group to effectively achieve a common purpose. Social capital can also be thought of as the potential ability to obtain resources, favors, or information from one's personal connections."[6] Social capital is what you are creating and earning through every interaction with your niche practice. Remember, when you have a focused law practice, you aren't seen as an outsider trying to get in. You are at the center; you have the necessary social capital; you are in.

---

[6] https://www.investopedia.com/terms/s/socialcapital.asp#:~:text=Social%20capital%20is%20a%20set,information%20from%20one's%20personal%20connections.

PREPARE YOUR MARKETING FOR YOUR SUCCESS

Connect Through Collateral

There will be many opportunities in the regular course of business for people to refer your legal services to others. It will be important to prepare your law firm marketing in advance of any visibility campaign in your niche market. Marketing collateral is anything digital or printed that you use to sell your legal services. Create marketing collateral that is reflective of your services for your clients to consume but also for professionals to share to accompany their referrals and keep them updated on your services.

Collateral Material Ideas

- Business cards
- One-page flyers
- Brochures
- Notecards, including thank you cards

Lawyers don't have to spend a ton of money when it comes to creating marketing collateral. In the past, you had to hire a writer and a graphic designer and outsource the printing to a local printer. This process has been modernized significantly, with design software being accessible to everyone and, most of the time, low cost to use. These design programs connect directly with online printing services, allowing your collateral materials to be printed on demand, changed or updated consistently, and then shipped directly to your door.

When developing materials related to your niche, consider marketing collateral from the perspective of the person sharing your information or buying your legal services. Ask yourself:

- Who is the audience for your collateral materials?
- What information will your audience of potential clients and referral sources need to know about your law practice and legal services that make them different from other options?

- When people contact your law firm, what kind of information would be helpful for them to receive about your legal services and the legal issues they are dealing with?
- Why will potential clients want to work with your law firm, and why will your referral sources want to refer your services to others?
- Where will the collateral materials be located—on your website, in printed form, or both?

Make the pathway clear for sharing information about your services and contacting your office. Again, reciprocated referrals are ideal, so you will want information from your professional network on how to share their contact information with your network as well.

Know the Players

Having a niche practice makes it easier to get to know the big players in a community. Your network in your niche practice will be a valuable resource for opportunities and exposure. Business-development-minded attorneys look to connect with others who have likewise earned the target audience's trust and respect. They know that a successful niche practice is not located on a one-way street. Personal relationships with others in a professional capacity should be dynamic, so they evolve, and trust deepens. These relationships are also reciprocal, so everyone benefits.

Finding a common purpose with other professionals who work in your focused market is simplified by looking at what is the same about what you do rather than what is different. Start to watch for repetitions, including repeated sponsorships by companies and frequent lectures by individuals. These people and organizations serve the same community that you do. Find ways to connect with them through social media backed up by in-person coffee or lunches. It is fine to ask for introductions whenever you can, as they create a warmer environment to connect and make it easier to work your way in. Be sure to learn about them and their offerings during these meetings, as ideas regarding collaboration to gain exposure together will follow. For example, the CPA has different services than yours, but their offerings support the health of a business, just like yours do from the legal side. In getting to know the players in an industry, focus on what is similar, not what is different. Your niche law practice can help you network by drilling down on the common solutions you provide to the target audience.

How to Stand Out to High-Value Contacts

1. **Clean up your online presence.** Do a Google search on your name and your law firm's name and delete any questionable or incorrect material you find. This includes personal social media profiles. If you intend to keep information online that your professional contacts will see, ensure that all of your privacy settings are adjusted to control who can see your content.
2. **Follow professional etiquette.** When you are preparing for an industry event in your niche, ensure that you have fresh, accurate business cards ready to hand out. Be sure to show interest in someone else's business card by looking at it before you put it in your bag. If you are sitting and someone walks up to introduce themselves, stand up with a smile and extend your hand.
3. **Create interest through value.** When you are in a niche, your interests will overlap with those of other professionals in your community. Finding ways to follow up with a high-value contact is made easier when you consider where you can educate, help, or even improve on something of common interest. Similarly, if you are reading articles and books in a shared subject, you can share that information with new contacts through an email after an event.

Additionally, visibility is easier in a niche, and genuine connections are made because you share a common focus. The situation is smaller in a niche market, so you can dive a bit more into your business relationships within this professional circle, finding ways to collaborate and connect with other professionals in the niche. Being as strategic as you are active in niche networking can build your community for you.

Credential Check

A niche will increase your practice's visibility. When the pond is smaller, you will be bigger. So, get to know the players in your focus area and find ways to be authentically involved. Look for organizations to join, boards to participate in, and even magazines to publish thought leadership through articles. Many organizations have blogs you can contribute to that will be provided to the exact audience you are trying to reach. The sum of these consistent activities, when kept within your niche, tells your story, builds your reputation, and provides you with the bulletproof credentials your target community needs to see.

Niche Marketing Considerations Regarding Attorney Biographies

- Short biographies are regularly needed for public speaking and sponsorships, and the longer version should be stored on your website. Keep a short-form biography (under 500 words) and a long-form biography handy in an editable format and keep them updated habitually, such as every quarter or every six months.
- When you are pounding the pavement doing business development and great legal work, your biography updating can fall to the wayside. Have an updating strategy for your biography that includes regular intervals for review by you or someone on your staff.
- Your most relevant information to your niche or audience should be apparent and included toward the beginning of your biography. You will want to focus on relevant qualifications, expertise, and experience. When you are focused on a niche, there will be aspects of your background that remain interesting but not necessarily pertinent to selling your legal services, such as law school awards.

By focusing on your niche and writing about it, speaking about it, and essentially knowing all there is to know, you become the go-to.

Your resume or CV provides a narrative of expertise through awards in your niche, publications in your focus area, and lectures on topics germane to your audience. This type of verifiable credibility becomes a unique selling point for your small firm law practice, and it clearly differentiates you from the competition. Reflect on how your legal services will fare in a beauty contest with another attorney at a bigger firm with a more general law practice. Your niche exhibits a comprehensive expertise alongside your target marketing that talks to your audience and their legal challenges. Your niche wins the new client.

A RETURN TO THE B2C SPOTLIGHT: FAMILY LAW NICHE PRACTICE

There might be hundreds of family law attorneys in your state or, depending on the size of your city, in your geographic area. However, maybe only a small percentage of the population provides legal services to Spanish-speaking families in their language.

A business development strategy backed by marketing activities for a lawyer looking to develop this type of niche practice could include providing articles that answer common questions about family law to the local Spanish-language newspaper. They could couple this strategy with well-placed ads in the same newspaper announcing webinars the law firm is hosting for the community in collaboration with a local church that provides services in Spanish. The attorney could seek out referral relationships with other Spanish-speaking attorneys who serve the same population for different reasons, such as criminal defense or personal bankruptcy lawyers. Oftentimes, these types of attorney-to-attorney relationships can lead to peer attorney awards that have eye-catching superlatives like "greatest" or "best" and "super."

(Continued)

A RETURN TO THE B2C SPOTLIGHT: FAMILY LAW NICHE PRACTICE *(CONTINUED)*

When this attorney looks back on their activities after six months or a year of collecting them on their biography, they are pleased to see that their credentials have taken shape, and they are well on their way to being a center of influence in their community through a niche practice.

Knowing your target audience well will help you customize your business development, personal marketing, and legal services to fit their needs. Be sure to collect feedback from your colleagues and clients, as testimonials validate that you are who you say you are. Your story will resonate with your audience because it was created specifically for them.

How to Dominate Your Niche

Level Up

Educating yourself in your niche is imperative. This will help you determine if a niche is a good fit for your practice and if profitability exists in this area. It will also help you understand your clients' challenges and what success looks like to your ideal audience. This educational process will feel like work because it is. Stating the obvious, it is hard to take non-billable time to learn about the niche subject matter, but remember, this is not all for naught. You are growing in a very specific and deliberate way as a professional. With every minute you spend attempting to understand your niche more, your law practice is being defined to support your career goals. When you are interested and passionate about a niche subject, you naturally want to share information about it, talk about it, and so on. This vested interest leads to ideas about programming and marketing needed.

Leveling up is an ongoing process, and once you decide on a focus for your practice, you must keep your saw sharp. The need to learn and keep yourself current in your niche doesn't end. The point of having a niche is so that your practice will grow alongside the community it serves.

Show Up

Developing a niche practice requires focused energy. You and your law firm will need to consistently show up in spaces where your ideal clients and referral sources are. It is important to recognize that showing up can look different for everyone, as there is not only one way to do it. For people who enjoy attending in-person events, showing up in their niche can mean attending scheduled happy hours, galas, and parties throughout the year. For those who are not as into face-to-face networking, it can mean a bigger push on social media within the niche market's preferred platforms and meeting new people in a targeted digital manner through Zoom follow-up calls.

GOOD THINKING

Body language conveys a lot about you to your audience in networking situations. If you are feeling upset, bored, or rushed, your body language will show it even if your words are trying to hide it. When you are meeting new connections, be sure to exhibit friendly body language and facial expressions, as studies find that "[e]ven something as simple as a handshake provides valuable first impressions for 72% of the people who do in-person meetings."[7]

Showing up consistently is not as easy as it sounds. How many of us put a 6 pm happy hour on our calendar, two weeks in advance, with every intention of attending—only to blow it off at the last minute? Be sure to make the time and space needed to commit to your goals as they relate to your niche.

---

[7] https://www.sciencedaily.com/releases/2019/04/190412094728.htm#google_vignette.

Follow-Up

There is no playbook for follow-up in a niche practice. The key is to find what activities work best for you and then stick to them. Following up with a new contact in your niche after an event might involve an email thanking them for their time, confirming how much you enjoyed meeting them, and that you would like to take them to lunch in a few weeks. That casual follow-up might be your speed. For others, a handwritten thank you note on branded marketing collateral might feel like a more personal touch. Following up politely with a customized LinkedIn connection request and message will also work well. Being polite and sincere in your messaging and method will set your solo or small law practice's follow-up apart from the competition. Be sure to brainstorm ways to stay in touch with the people you are meeting in your niche, including adding them to your law firm newsletter, as well as scheduling a coffee in a few weeks or a lunch next quarter. The point of follow-up is to stay visible with the people you are trying so hard to meet in your niche. The methods you choose to use are entirely up to you.

REAL-WORLD ETHICS

Small law firm attorneys can fall into using misleading marketing statements that make their marketing more competitive or persuasive but also operate in a grey area. For example, a new litigation and trial practice law firm owned by three seasoned litigators with established careers might be tempted to combine their experience. These attorneys recognize that while their law firm is new, their law practices are not, so they proudly state their combined 30 years of litigation experience on their website and in collateral materials. Through this statement, they intend to offset any perceived nascence in their law firm with the confirmation of decades of combined experience. *However, these attorneys should check the rules regarding marketing in each state they are licensed to ensure compliance.* In real-world marketing and business development, there will be many opportunities to inflate or exaggerate your small or solo law firm's experience or results. If you are actively building your practice and taking notes on your successes, big and small, for your clients, you will create a truthful story about your firm that you can market proudly and ethically.

***

Matching your legal services to consumers' needs is key to creating and generating demand for a niche law practice. Driving this awareness and interest in your law practice starts with a complete understanding of your audience and their needs, wants, and desires. Knowing what is important to them makes it easier for your law practice to reach and engage with the right people at the right moment or through the right messaging.

Some attorneys stumble on a niche or a focus, and others set out intentionally to have it. Even if your law firm doesn't have many previous or current clients in a niche yet, a deliberate plan to pursue a focus with the actions to back it up starts you on a path to intentionally attracting this work to your firm.

A niche allows you to focus your marketing and business development on your exact audience. By figuring out where they are, what they read, and even what podcasts they listen to, the law firm can learn more about its ideal client. This can lead to insight into where to network, which events to sponsor, and the type of advertisement and messaging needed for long-term business development success. A niche can be an aspect of your law practice or encompass the entire focus. Regardless of its size, a niche practice is focused and memorable and helps you attract the work to your practice that you desire. A niche puts you at the center of a community or the center of an industry because you are trusted to handle their legal issues.

2

Character

> ***Your brand is what people say about you when you are not in the room.***
>
> **—Jeff Bezos**

In this chapter, we work through personal branding and its place in business development for solo and small law firm lawyers. A great personal brand is a key factor driving the visibility and memorability of a law practice. In business development, personal branding done right can give small law firm attorneys an advantage over bigger teams and marketing budgets. This chapter provides attorneys with information on how to develop their personal brand to increase visibility while building trust through credentialed expertise. A strong personal brand positions small law firm attorneys as authorities, improving their practice's competitiveness, boosting confidence, and attracting potential clients and referral sources.

***

Your brand is how people perceive you, see you, and remember you. What's brilliant about personal branding for attorneys is that it is all in their control. You get to develop the memorable character of your law firm. Your brand should reflect your interests, passions, education, and credentials. It is your story and an impression of what you bring to the table. Your brand makes it easy for you to be remembered, included, and invited.

WHAT IS PERSONAL BRANDING FOR LAWYERS?

In a nutshell, your personal brand is what you want other people to know about you, think about you, and say about you. A personal brand gives recognizable legs to a law practice regardless of size. And as the Jeff Bezos quote suggests, it will speak for you when you aren't in the room. Personal brand is hard to define but can be summarized as "the combination of your skills, the values you present, and the impression you leave on others."[1] With a focused and genuine brand, people understand your career goals as a lawyer and why you are passionate about them. A personal brand is another way to make marketing and business development decisions easier on you, as you can say "yes" or "no" depending on whether it works with your branding goals and strategy. Your personal brand will help you gain visibility and be recognized in your niche. Branding yourself makes you more memorable because you stand out in a curated way. It can also help define and direct your legal career and, if it matters, give you mobility.

DO YOU NEED A PERSONAL BRAND?

Many successful attorneys have given me pushback on the need for a personal brand and a branded legal career. They are adamant that they have climbed to the top of the mountain and experienced professional success without one. I disagree. Even if you haven't intentionally pursued a personal brand in your career, if you are

---

[1] https://hbr.org/2023/09/how-to-define-develop-and-communicate-your-personal-brand.

successful, *you have a brand*. Even if you don't feed your personal brand through a strategy, formal or informal, and you are well-known in your community, *you have a brand*. Effective attorneys stand for something or support something. Memorable lawyers have a defined side or stance. Successful attorneys have a strong narrative or story that propels them and draws people into their circle. All this chatter is backed up by strong expertise, experience, and results in their practice areas. Pull that all together, and *you have a brand*.

Developing a personal brand is about developing others' perceptions of you. It's about *them*, what *they* think, what *they* remember, and what *they* share with others when referring potential clients to your legal services. Your audience can help you find your personal brand based on the trust and help that you bring into their world.

What's exciting about a personal brand is that it is dynamic and can change to reflect your growth as a professional. Maybe you started your legal career as a public defender, and that work helped give direction to your career and was propelled by your core beliefs. You were focused on being a part of securing justice in the criminal defense system as much as you possibly could. Maybe your personal brand changed organically when you moved into private practice, and as a business owner/lawyer you continued to be guided by your internal compass, pointing you toward the defense of others and the protection of their rights just in the private sector.

Your personal brand can and will change as your career progresses. If you are authentic about your core mission, your values, and how you serve your community, your personal brand will naturally adjust to accommodate your future and growth. It will also be a differentiator for your law practice regardless of how crowded the market is. In business development, personal branding done right can give solo and small law firm attorneys an advantage over bigger teams with bigger budgets. Regardless of whether building a brand has been an active process, successful lawyers have one. So, to answer the question of whether you need a personal brand? Yes.

B2B SPOTLIGHT: BRANDING IN BUSINESS LAW

Years ago, I worked with a business lawyer who wanted to be known as a"problem solver"in the business community. Pursuing a personal brand as a problem solver doesn't happen overnight. It requires a blend of community trust, intentional activities, and notable experience—basically being a problem solver isn't something that you can walk into. It requires work, and here is how we did it.

Working with this attorney to develop a personal brand started with determining what exactly his offering was to the community. We looked at his network, which was vast. He had stayed connected and in good standing with the key players in the city in top industries. We also gathered a written list of his past experiences in different scenarios, finding solutions and solving problems for others. A review of his internal and external processes revealed that most of the time, there was a light pattern of how he helped; activating his network by engaging the right people who had the social capital or insight to fix problems was usually involved in the resolution.

It was clear that his personal brand had been taking shape for years through consistent trust-based networking. People in different communities turned to him for help as his problem-solving skills went outside the box, and the community knew that. All this research into the results of his practice while taking stock of his results in handling complex problems for others helps us direct his branded business development.

We sketched out a plan for him to deepen connections with the people he already knew. We did this while strategically getting in front of decision-makers who had the authority to purchase his legal services when they had big or bad issues to solve. The consistency in his behavior and results for years led to an easy launching point to do better business development under the catchy and branded notoriety of being a"problem solver."

BRAINSTORM YOUR BRAND

When it comes to marketing, we always start in our own backyard. The soul searching for personal branding can begin with open-ended questions:

- Why did you go to law school, and how did you keep those promises to yourself?
- What types of engagements or clients make you feel the best?
- What makes you better qualified to help a certain demographic or with a certain legal issue?
- What would you love to be true about yourself in the next year to five years?
- What will the personal brand accomplish for your law firm's reputation?

The answers to these questions can be jotted down in a journal or typed in the notes section of your computer. There is no right way to start this deep dive into what you want to be known for professionally. This effort is going to feel deeply personal because it is.

The personal branding process zigzags for everyone. That assurance is critical because there will be times when you turn left instead of right or when you pursue something shiny that comes up. Most of us are a bit flakey at times, especially when it comes to our own goals. But your personal brand will always be based on the impression you leave and the reputation you have earned and maintained. You shape your brand—your values, value, and consistent activity—but it is based on your audience and what they say and think about you. Your brand is determined by your goals, current and future. So, as they say, dress for the job you want, not the job you have. Look at

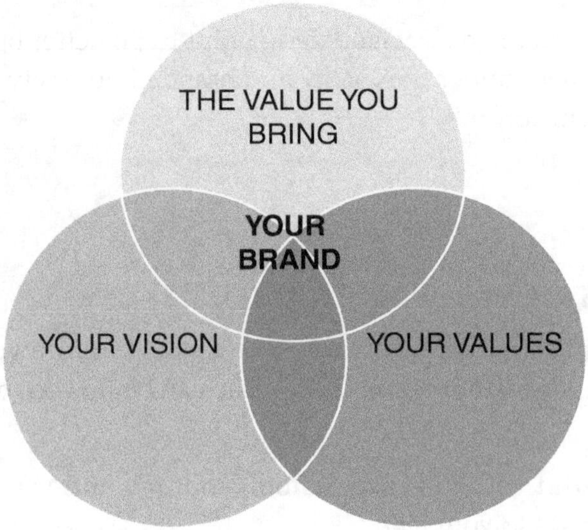

Figure 2.1 Venn Diagram.

this process holistically and forward thinking, as it is a blend of your beliefs and behaviors that create a personal brand.

Regardless of what you choose to focus on in your personal branding, you will want to be consistent and authentic. This will create confidence in you, and this trust will build connections for your law practice. Branding starts with your value, your values, and your vision (Figure 2.1). The mix of these aspects of your law practice will help you create your personalized message.

Your Value

Your value is who you are and what you bring to the table when it comes to your audience of potential clients and referral sources. To be very clear, your value is not a description of what you do for a living, but rather how you help and serve your community through your legal practice and what type of help that provides to your audience.

For example, if you are a B2B transactional real estate lawyer, your value might be centered around your high-level knowledge of the real estate industry, which you apply to your cases to recognize and avoid risk while providing legal services that support your clients' bigger goals. This is different from a B2C criminal defense attorney who brings value to their community by protecting the rights of citizens accused of crimes in a cost-effective, approachable, and zealous manner.

Your Values

Your values, on the other hand, are summarized as your core principles, what personally matters to you. Your professional values might center around securing justice for others and having integrity in your law practice. Your professional values might include your commitment to respecting the planet and sustainability through providing the "greenest" legal services you can possibly provide. For others, their professional values will focus on a foundation of respect and collaboration in their law firm's legal services.

The values behind your legal practice are important, and they have bigger effects on your practice than you might realize.

- Your values will guide decisions on what types of client engagements are a good fit for your law practice and which aren't.
- They can help you decide on the type of office space your firm will be in or which neighborhood.
- Professional values shape your career by providing boundaries to make decisions.
- Having professional values at the forefront of your law practice keeps your career aligned with your foundational mission and goals.

Your Vision

Vision is the next component of your personal brand. I am sure you have been around lawyers whom you admire for a variety of reasons. But if you look carefully at what you like or want to emulate in your own career, their distinctiveness probably relates back to their vision for their career. It is easy to want to be at the top of the profession, but if you look at what it took to get to the top, you can see the outline of their vision.

A vision for your law practice is the legacy, impact, and reputation that you want to secure. Your vision is your end goal, and it must be present in the decisions you make regarding business development and marketing. Sample career visions for lawyers can include paid corporate board membership, key types of client engagements, authoring a book in their niche, or providing impactful case results. For others, the vision might include personal visibility or credentialing, such as securing the cover of a magazine or being consistently in headline news.

GOOD THINKING

A career vision is as organic as it is dynamic. It can and will change over time. Attorneys who adopt a growth mindset when it comes to professional success will thrive with this uncertainty. A growth mindset is a tool and a belief that "their talents can be developed (through hard work, good strategies, and input from others)."[2] A growth mindset helps professionals overcome obstacles and stay committed to their values even when experiencing challenges or setbacks in their business development.

There also will be different periods of career development, and some transitions cannot be accounted for in advance. Your vision as a component of your personal brand will include your values and answers to a fundamental question—at the end of your career, what do you want to be true? Or a less daunting question, what do you want to be true in the next two years? Putting the value, values, and vision together creates your law practice's unique personal brand.

---

[2] https://hbr.org/2016/01/what-having-a-growth-mindset-actually-means.

FOUNDATIONAL CONSIDERATIONS FOR YOUR PERSONAL BRAND

A personal brand shows your character and is based on authenticity and consistency. It helps showcase what you value in yourself, in others, and in society. As discussed earlier, branding will come to reflect your community's expectations of you. What is empowering about all this is that your brand is entirely up to you.

The word "foundation" is used intentionally here. You will construct your brand. The value, values, and vision are at the foundation of the branding strategy that you are creating. They inform additional aspects of your brand that only deepen its memorability. Through personal branding, solo and small law firm attorneys will have a connected and more deliberate approach to business development.

#1: Your Value Proposition

Regardless of the number of lawyers, a law firm is a for-profit business that needs to sell legal services. Your value proposition is a commitment to your target audience about how you solve their problems, meet their goals, or secure successful results for them. Your value proposition is a statement that informs potential clients or referral sources about your services. It must be succinct and specific. Through your value proposition, you have the space of a nutshell to communicate why your legal services meet their needs and address their issues. If cost considerations or even demographic information matter to your audience, you can include them in your value proposition. Savvy attorneys address their audience's pain points and include their own practice differentiators to substantiate their value proposition when possible.

SAMPLE VALUE PROPOSITION FOR A SOLO LAW FIRM
My law firm supports families in transition by providing cost-effective divorce and family law legal services in Spanish.

SAMPLE VALUE PROPOSITION FOR A SMALL LAW FIRM

Our firm's attorneys support individuals and families in financial crises through our personalized and cost-conscious bankruptcy legal services.

To be very clear, your value proposition is an aspect of your personal brand or your small law firm's brand. It is not a tagline or a slogan. Your value proposition is a succinct way of communicating to your audience and referral sources what your law practice does for others. When you nail your value proposition, you cultivate your public persona by defining and expressing a coherent narrative about your law practice. This statement is as personal as it is public. It lives on your website home page, in your electronic and printed brochures, and might be involved in how you introduce yourself to new connections. A survey produced by the ABA found that "[t]hirty-two percent of respondents had clients retain them through their website, including 36% of both solos and respondents in firms of 10–49 lawyers, and 39% of lawyers in firms of 2–9 lawyers."[3] This data drives home the fact that your website is a great tool to showcase aspects of your personal brand to help you connect with your intended audience and convert leads to clients.

#2: Emotional Connection

The American Psychological Association gives a great definition of what can feel like an undefinable and unseen force that is present in everyone's decision of whether to purchase legal services from an attorney—emotions. They state, "Emotions are conscious mental reactions (such as anger or fear) subjectively experienced as strong

[3] https://www.americanbar.org/groups/law_practice/resources/legal-technology-resource-center/tech-survey/2020/.

feelings usually directed toward a specific object and typically accompanied by physiological and behavioral changes in the body."[4] Although they are hard to quantify or explain, emotional connections are among the purest forms of communication we can make with others. This is true even in a law practice.

When you are developing your personal brand, consider the emotions associated with your legal services. For example, one of the strongest emotions that can be invoked in others is love and all that is associated with it, including positivity, happiness, and satisfaction. How can your personal brand speak to the love that compels parents to invest thousands of dollars on a trust and estate plan that will protect their children's futures? On the B2B side, speaking to the emotional side of a business transaction might include exhibiting authenticity and trust. When you are firm in showcasing your values and expertise, you are communicating your brand. Do it consistently and intentionally, and you are well on your way to an authentic personal brand for your law practice. Having an emotional component to your brand will help you stand out from others through a uniqueness that is alive and productive in your business development.

B2C SPOTLIGHT: A LAWYER WITH A FAMOUS PERSONAL BRAND

One of my favorite examples of a lawyer with a great personal brand is Gloria Allred. Ms. Allred is powerful and prominent in the media. She is known for taking on civil cases involving women, especially women in unjust situations and uphill battles. Her cases are controversial, and she doesn't fear high-profile opponents. Ms. Allred is the one you hire when you need to fight hard.

Ms. Allred wasn't born holding press conferences to powerfully advocate for others. She also isn't genetically

(Continued)

[4] https://www.apa.org/topics/emotions.

B2C SPOTLIGHT: A LAWYER WITH A FAMOUS PERSONAL BRAND *(CONTINUED)*

predetermined to be the most visible lawyer in the room. What the world remembers about Gloria Allred's brand and what they admire about the high-profile client engagements she attracts—she built.

The values behind her practice are as clear as the type of client she represents. She is an activist, feminist, *and a civil lawyer.*

She advocates for gender equality while sharply criticizing individuals and industries that perpetuate discrimination, *and she is a civil lawyer.*

Her brand is a master class in consistently communicating a personal brand tied to authentic emotions and next-level legal results. Ms. Allred has a powerfully coherent branding strategy that has shaped people's expectations and beliefs about her. She wove her true self into a personal brand, and she maintains a consistent passion for the issues that fuel her civil law practice.

Emotions are important attributes that feed directly into the memorability and longevity of your personal brand. Emotional connections are linked to how you want people to feel about your law practice. They include bravery in your criminal defense work and trust in your business law practice. Your personal brand as a family law attorney may include calm and understanding attributes. A litigator might want to be associated with positive emotions like relief and calmness in stressful situations. When you are thinking of your personal brand, focus on the blend of what you want to be known for and what traits will resonate with your client base. Put yourself in their shoes to better understand what would feel good to hear about their lawyer at this moment or what type of personal characteristics would be ideal for you to bring to the table in their legal situation.

#3: Sharing Your Brand

Figuring out how to announce your personal brand doesn't have to be a challenge or even an "announcement." When it comes to exhibiting and sharing your brand, you will need to determine what channels you will use to provide frequent, reliable content that underscores what you do to help and serve your community. A review of your potential client base's demographics reveals patterns regarding gender, occupation, location, education level, and even income. These data points shed insight into the people who need your legal services. The data also helps you match up your services with their challenges. After you listen to that community to learn what makes them tick, you can create a brand that sets you up for success.

Sharing your brand will include determining how you will appear on the social media platforms that your audience engages with. For some, this will look like the frequency of Instagram posts coupled with in-app advertisements. For others, it can look like funnel building through long-form blog writing on LinkedIn that leads back to gated content on their website. It can also involve being introduced to media outlets such as newspapers, TV programs, and blogs that are important to your potential clients. It is interesting to note that an ABA survey found "46% of lawyers with their own legal topic blog report at least one client has retained them as a result of their legal topic blog."[5] Don't discount the power of your own website when it comes to branding.

Sharing your brand will look different for everyone and most attorneys can use their own media including websites and LinkedIn pages to communicate brand. At the beginning of your branding process, it can take the form of a sketch or an outline of the ways that you want to connect with your audience. As time goes on, that outline will take better shape to become a key part of your marketing plan that works together with your business development.

---

[5] https://www.americanbar.org/groups/law_practice/resources/legal-technology-resource-center/tech-survey/2020/.

#4: The Long Game

Developing a strong foundation for your personal brand requires thinking long term, especially regarding the behavior and activities that will support your brand goals. The legal industry is innately competitive, and the work required to build a reputation can be destroyed in one bad week or even one bad moment.

If you want to establish a foothold in a certain industry or with a certain group, show up. You should be networking with them, lecturing to them, and writing articles for their publications. You should know what they are saying and what they are reading because you are a part of their community. The trust from your community that supports your personal brand comes from consistency in activity.

The trust from your community also comes from consistency in your demeanor. People will remember how you treat them—always. One bad day or one bad interaction with you can stay with you, regardless of how you try to make it better. A negative interaction outweighs a positive one, and it can overshadow anything good you are trying to be a part of.

Chances are the communities you are involved in, especially your legal community, feel bigger than they actually are. It is easy to develop a brand within the legal community. It is also smart to develop a brand in the legal community, because in this industry, you never know where the next career opportunity or great case referral will come from. When you have a personal brand that is working for you, you protect it. This will include having a long-game plan on how you want to be thought of in the legal community. What will people say about you when you aren't in the room? Are you smart and great at what you do but rude and difficult to work with? Are you easy to work with and fantastic at what you do but show up late to every meeting?

A personal brand will help build resilience in your law practice, and there is long-term work to maintaining a brand. You will have to stay on top of trends, giving you an edge when it comes to thought leadership. You might need to speak at conferences and events as much as you attend them. You will need to seek out other players in your industry to figure out how to collaborate to bring new solutions and creativity to your area of expertise. From the extra effort you are expending, you will be better than most at what you do, and it will show. But when you are rushed, stressed, or upset, take a minute to remember that your one bad day or that one nasty email you sent can neutralize positive branding efforts.

LAYERING YOUR BRAND

Once you have a general idea of your personal brand, bringing it to life is an exercise in layering activities and expertise.

Branding Through Activities and Organizations

Your practice area can align with your personal brand in many visible ways, including supporting other organizations in the same field or doing pro bono work. Similarly, a lawyer who donates a portion of their fees back to a popular nonprofit that serves the same population as their law firm can brand through that alignment.

For example, you want to be known as the "go-to" attorney for plaintiff personal injury in your area, so you align with organizations that focus on safe driving or programs that support people regaining their health after catastrophic injuries. Being active in these organizations will help you credential your career and strengthen your brand. After all, you are not just talking the talk by putting information on a billboard like your competitors; you are in the community through service. You are walking the walk.

Pro bono matters can also have legs when it comes to personal branding in the solo and small firm world. Pro bono engagements can be hard to take on in a smaller shop but are not impossible. This is another area of your career where your intention can inform your activities. Pro bono work comes in all shapes and sizes. It can be through existing organizations, small engagements, part of a case, a co-counsel relationship, devoted time to legal nights, and so on. Adding *pro bono* work to your strategy doesn't have to be a time and money pit. If your intention is to help people through donated work, there are large and small ways to do so.

B2B SPOTLIGHT: BRANDING THROUGH PRO BONO PROJECTS

A small or solo B2B law firm can take on a pro bono project for a client or even many pro bono projects throughout the year. However, if its heart is in the right place, but its marketing isn't, it doesn't get credit for the good it is doing in the community.

A B2B law firm that actively solicits small pro bono projects throughout the year must have a follow-up plan on how they will share information about this aspect of their firm with their audience. This can look like case studies, scrubbed of personal information, posted on the law firm's website, included in their email campaign, and sprinkled out as LinkedIn posts. Likewise, the follow-up marketing plan to pro bono work can include requesting testimonials from pro bono clients on the firm's Google My Business page. Their testimonial isn't mandated but rather a way to show their appreciation for the help with, for example, entity formation for their small business. They can steer away from specifics in the testimonial and focus on the client services, the emotions, and what the results meant to them.

Pro bono can be valuable in branding as part of a business development and marketing strategy if there is intention and if there is a plan.

Branding Through Credentialing

Personal branding is a form of promotion that can take you from relative obscurity to what will feel like fame. However, as we have discussed, it takes work. Your brand will be shaped by the blend of what you say and what you do, including all the professional activities you are involved in. Your personal brand can incorporate awards and honors in the area where you wish to be known.

GOOD THINKING

Attorneys working on their personal brand find that the visibility associated with deliberate branding, including joining committees and championing causes, will tee them up for awards and honors aligned with their brand. Peer-generated awards from bar associations, Super Lawyers®, and Best Lawyers in America® are a great way to build a solo or small law firm's presence. These awards can align with your practice areas or niche offerings, giving an additional credential to your law practice; they also provide great fodder for email marketing and social media announcements.

Skill development and personal development might be necessary to accelerate your brand. For some, new skills might be necessary to move to the next level of leadership. For others, it might be more education in a certain area, and so they need to go after an extra certification to credential their law practice. There are also opportunities to engage in micro-credentialing that lets you better understand an industry or an issue. For example, a white-collar lawyer might consider taking a few accounting classes to understand their basic principles better and make their legal advice more informed.

Personal branding through credentialing also includes awards and honors. These types of accolades feel good and make your law firm look good. They provide line items for your website bio through third-party validation, content for blog and social media posting, and branded updates to your CV. Having an intact personal brand keeps your career alive and mobile. It opens doors by helping to tell a story about you.

To return to the B2C example of the plaintiff personal injury attorney looking to create a personal brand, that attorney might donate a portion of all awarded fees toward educating the community on texting and driving issues. They might combine this donation with a few *pro bono* legal clinics where they teach the community tips on how to advocate for themselves in situations involving insurance companies. After years of consistent donations through time and money, the attorney receives a plaque from the community acknowledging their contributions. This plaque can be displayed in the law firm's lobby or main conference room. It can also be photographed for the firm's website. The addition of a personal brand, in this example, amplifies the plaintiff's personal attorney's reputation in the community as a leader and a person working toward making it better for everyone rather than someone looking to collect a portion of a settlement check.

Although everyone's end goal with credentialing is different, all strategies should include increased visibility for their law practice. For people to know about your law practice, they need to be exposed to it. Visibility is another tool in your marketing and business development toolbox. Visibility for attorneys can be seen through credentialing activities such as publishing articles and participating in pieces where they were interviewed as subject matter experts by local publications. Visibility through branded credentialing can be pursued through interviews on podcasts that are related to your personal brand in some way. It can be pursued by event attendance and event sponsorship. There are lots of ways to support your brand through credentialing activities, but ensuring that the activities you are involved in are aligned with your personal brand continues to build on your law practice's credibility.

Branding Through Client Engagements

The types of projects and engagements that your firm takes on can align with your personal brand. Branding through client engagements is a result of deliberate marketing and business development with individuals and mission-based organizations.

A personal brand has more teeth when it shows action in the community. Lawyers often learn about large cases that they can be involved in through existing watchdog organizations such as the ACLU. They can catch the case before it is filed or even request to join the trial team after it is filed to strengthen support for the issue at hand. Having a small part in a larger case can be satisfying on a personal level while supporting the brand backing up your business development.

INCLUDING INCLUSION

If you want a personal brand aligned with promoting diversity, equity, and inclusion (DEI), the end goal might be to be a change agent in your law firm, in the legal community, and in the careers of diverse professionals. When you reverse engineer that goal, to be known for DEI work, you need to start being involved in these programs and initiatives. It might start with a conversation with someone who is already involved in these programs or even a cursory online search for what is new or interesting to be involved in.

An attorney looking to develop a personal brand related to DEI might join groups centered around these issues. They could eventually have a larger goal of starting their own program or initiative. An attorney that has this personal brand would be interested in recruiting diverse attorneys to work in their own law firm, and they might have diverse attorneys on their short-list for referrals in areas of law that they don't practice in.

Having a DEI-centered personal brand supports postings about DEI topics and issues on professional social media profiles, such as LinkedIn. They might aggregate DEI news and write short comments about an issue on their social media post, showing interest, thought leadership, and understanding of DEI in the community. A DEI-focused brand could lead to writing articles for their law firm's newsletter with information about DEI consistently, along with writing articles externally for local news sources on DEI topics.

The example shows the intention and consistency needed to develop a strong personal brand related to DEI. It can be done by yourself as a solo practitioner or as part of a small law firm. The size of the firm will determine the resources available to pursue the brand, but there are many avenues that can be pursued through the intentional use of two resources that we all have—time and effort. The big picture understanding is that personal branding doesn't just happen; it doesn't just show up one day in a wrapped package on your doorstep. Branding is a process that takes strategy backed up by effort and intention.

DEEPENING YOUR PERSONAL BRAND

Your personal brand is not static. It is a dynamic and interesting part of how you present yourself to your community. They say what you water grows, and it is important to give your personal brand ways to develop. Through a variety of activities within a cause or a community, actionable ways to continue to cultivate and strengthen your brand after it is initially established will naturally come up.

When you are starting or deepening a personal brand, you start at a familiar place: a bit of research. You look for the holes, look for what is wrong along with what is right. You note if a group is being underserved or underrepresented. This type of research reveals where value can be added: more specifically, where you and your law practice can add value. The process of frequent learning about your audience will layer your brand with knowledge.

Connecting with others through personal branding includes big and small contributions to the community you are looking to support. For example, a small business law firm could aim to help in a big way by collectively transforming an industry with new ideas on how to handle old legal problems. This effort to deepen their brand is bigger than that of a solo business attorney who wants to be known only for protecting their clients by putting sharper claws in their contracts. These examples show that branding goals are both micro and macro. They are uniquely personal to the individual, and adding dimensions to your brand, regardless of their size, will lead to more growth and consistency in your law practice.

Layering your brand shouldn't be difficult, as it is based in activities that are part of your greater business development strategy. Returning to the example of the attorney who wants to be known for promoting DEI in the community, maybe they serve others by being an ally to minority communities or diverse attorneys. They layer their brand by serving women in business through intentional work with the local chamber of commerce. They might also be known for career sponsorship and mentorship of younger lawyers from minority backgrounds. Another lawyer with a B2B practice might want to be known for being involved in cutting-edge industries or projects. To be known as innovative, they might be involved in business incubators or helping start-ups through existing small business organizations. They might write for this community through their law firm website blog and contributions to the business incubator's newsletter.

There is no step-by-step playbook for deepening your personal brand by adding dimensions. But you need to point all of your branded activities in the same direction, so the same narrative is being told. Developing your professional image will be unique to you, your practice, and your circumstances, including resources and audience. What will be true for everyone is the ability to look for places where you can be of service, but what you do with those opportunities will be up to you.

DRIVING DEMAND TOWARD YOUR PERSONAL BRAND

Your personal brand is a way for people to connect with you on a more memorable level. Personal branding for attorneys allows your audience to have a general sense of what you bring to the table. It is a tool for you to use to connect with your audience. Through personal branding, you insert trust and authority into your law practice and boost your lead-generation strategy. But you cannot be everything to everyone, so you will want to pick only a few topics that you want to focus on—in my opinion, three topics max that relate back to how you serve the community through your practice.

Career success in a certain area is backed up by a clear demand strategy focused on what you want to do more of or the impact that you want your professional life to have on others. A cursory review of the news will reveal what is going on in society at any given moment. But looking at the news headlines through the lens of your personal brand helps you see the media content that aligns with your audience or their issues. Look for patterns, themes, and trends in the news, as this is an idea bank. The local, national, and international news is a great starting place for social media content for your law firm, generating blogging ideas, and uncovering topics for article pitches that you can write or be quoted in. When reviewing the local and national news headlines, you can also look for ideas to deepen your personal brand from within the legal community. In law, there are industry-specific topics that can easily be included within a lawyer's personal brand. Great examples are seen in issues that constantly need to be addressed in the legal industry, such as DEI and mentoring.

REAL WORLD ETHICS

Nothing tests your patience as much as seeing a bad online review or something negative written about you or your law firm published by an angry client. While it is true that customer feedback has always been a part of doing business or owning a law firm, these days, it feels a little more personal. There are many options for people to vent online about lawyers, warranted or not. Law firms have little support when dealing with online review issues through major search algorithms and social media platforms. They want to be seen as neutral in these situations, and so they largely stay out of disputes. But you cannot afford to put your head in the sand as a solo or small law firm attorney when faced with negative feedback online. These online reviews and how you respond to them are part of your image and brand. Online reputation management is essential for solo and small law firms to stay competitive. I have seen attorneys lifted by their community through positive feedback in online reviews. I have also seen excellent lawyers and their law firms bombarded with negative online reviews by one angry former client. It works both ways.

When you receive an online review, give yourself time to process it. Is there anything in it that is true, accurate, or fair? Attorneys who are savvy businesspeople consider areas of growth when they receive such feedback from clients. They will also correct what they can fix if it is easy or obvious. However, your ethics and professionalism can be tested when the reviews aren't fair or truthful. Attorneys who respond angrily in the face of a negative online review only escalate the situation. *In facing a negative review or online comment about your law firm, be sure to review the rules regarding communication and marketing in the states where you are admitted to ensure compliance.*

Online reviews are a part of doing business in solo and small firms. If you can't change the game, you can at least get better at playing it. Consider the following ideas on how to handle online reviews consistently:

- Monitor your online accounts where clients can leave reviews, such as Google and Facebook business pages, Martindale-Hubbell, Yelp, and AVVO. Set up a calendared reminder or engage a third party to help you stay on schedule when reviewing your online presence.
- Respond thoughtfully to all client reviews, positive and negative. In responding to online reviews, consider the perspective of your potential clients and referral sources. Remember, these reviews can significantly influence their decision to work with you. In your response to positive or even glowing feedback about your legal services, be polite, gracious, and humble. This is also true in your response to negative reviews—be civil.
- Maintain client confidentiality in your response. Your client is not bound by the same ethical guidelines you are. Lawyers who take the bait and get into a back-and-forth argument with their former clients through an online review platform do a disservice to their business. While it feels satisfying to defend yourself when you see the online review pop up, remember that public disagreements with clients don't age well. Always keep your response polite and high level. By taking the issue offline as much as possible, you can be in control and proactive, offering a telephone call or a meeting to discuss the matter further.

***

Developing your personal brand makes your law practice mission driven. It makes your audience, whatever it is—individual clients or companies—understand what you can do for them and why they should hire you. Having a brand makes it easier for people to get on board with what you are doing; it helps you cement your relationship long-term. Developing your personal brand can also allow you to have a bigger seat at the table—whether that be in the legal community or in the local community. Having a personal brand allows you to understand a situation enough to look for big challenges and tackle them. Everything related to your personal brand will feed into the way you are perceived, known, and remembered by others. Having a solid personal brand quickly takes you from "Who are you?" to "How are you?"

3

Circles

> *You can close more business in two months by becoming interested in other people than you can in two years by trying to get people interested in you.*
>
> **—Dale Carnegie**

This chapter provides insight into finding opportunities within professional organizations and how to vet future potential communities to join. Consistent and branded activity in professional communities helps small law firms increase the market share of visibility and referrals to their practice. Many small law firm attorneys aren't instructed on vetting professional organizations, including bar associations, for business development opportunities. The benefits of joining and participating in professional organizations are immense for small law firms. They can include access to business development and marketing opportunities in addition to providing peer support and camaraderie.

***

I can't tell you how many attorneys I have spoken with about their business development efforts who physically cringe at the thought of networking with other attorneys. I have heard over and over how different they are from everyone else in law and why they can't stand "X, Y, and Z" about the profession. The gripes about the legal industry are predictable (and oftentimes warranted when looking at an individual level). There are many social dynamics at play in the legal community, as a microcosm of our larger community, that cause disconnect between attorneys. So I get it; going to a concert with friends and going to a bar association happy hour are not equal amounts of fun. Business development networking commitments and social efforts need to be viewed differently from those that are just plain relaxing. But one definitely has more long-term value for your business development. You should make room in your life for both.

Not including professional associations and other lawyers in your business development means you are missing out on networking with one of the most abundant sources for referrals to your law firm. Avoiding other attorneys as a practicing attorney is simply shortsighted. Successful lawyers are part of at least one professional community. Super-successful attorneys are part of a few communities, one of which is always the legal community—a bold statement that I can back up many times over.

Widening your circle to include professional community engagement, especially to involve other attorneys, helps capture more visibility and market share with your target audience or industry. Being a part of a professional community deepens your law practice through a better understanding of the people, topics, and issues your law practice handles. Professional community engagement also helps a law practice gain visibility in the audiences that they want to help and serve through their legal services. It builds trust with schools, neighborhoods, and groups through a shared common goal. A small law firm with an established community presence is more likely to connect with community members because it feels organic and less forced.

For some, local and national bar associations offer fellowship and camaraderie in addition to case referrals. Others find their place in specialty bar associations attached to minority groups or practice areas that allow them to access a community of attorneys with a smaller footprint or connect through very specific common ground, such as ethnicity or language. Regardless of your practice area, consistent activity in professional groups, including professional groups in the legal industry, will heighten your business development efforts.

REASONS TO JOIN A PROFESSIONAL COMMUNITY

The reasons to seek out a professional community for your law practice are immense. The data found in a Clio Trends Report makes it clear that "59% of clients seek a lawyer referral" from someone in their network rather than finding legal help on their own.[1] Professional communities and the networking they bring to your practice are a must-do. You only get referrals from other lawyers if they know who you are and how you practice. On a personal level, it doesn't have to be agonizing to attend professional events, and, in an ideal world, it is a bit of fun to be involved. Widening your circle widens your lens, personally and professionally, through participation that benefits your solo or small law firm's business development.

> **GOOD THINKING**
>
> ***Your circle can include professional groups that center around volunteering or pro bono work. Being in the service of others goes behind altruism and is good for your health and well-being. There are many positive mental and physical benefits associated with volunteering—one report suggests that people who volunteer over 100 hours per year are some of the healthiest people in our country.***[2]

---

[1] https://www.clio.com/resources/legal-trends/2019-report/.

[2] https://www.americorps.gov/.

Volunteering is good for you and good for your law practice. Professional communities, like bar associations, encourage personal growth through participation in educational events and networking. Done right, your involvement in a professional organization becomes an "easy button" for you to push when looking to determine where you can spend your business development energy for the maximum return. There are opportunities to gain new connections to add to your LinkedIn profile or take photos for your marketing while volunteering with a group doing something that feels good to be a part of. When you choose the activities to engage in as closely as you choose the organization, the result is a good mix of business development and fun.

These groups also provide opportunities to grow professionally. I see many attorneys leveling up their CVs through leadership roles in local and national bar associations. Through line-item entries on their biographies about their roles in bar associations, they share insight with their audience about their personal accountability and professional commitment to being the best lawyer they can be in their area of specialty.

Professional organizations in the legal industry are not just bar associations; they are also fellowships and inns of court. There are legal foundations, nonprofits, and law firms that have practice areas focused on public interest causes. They are normally founded based on something in common, such as geography, or an area of law. These organizations promote the public good through access to legal services, justice for underrepresented groups, or protecting property or individual rights. Having a shared value system or commitment to a cause with an organization makes it easier for solo and small law firms to engage with these types of circles. They can more easily find groups that align with their audience, goals, or vision for their law practice.

In addition to legal industry organizations, small firm attorneys have a variety of options when it comes to finding communities outside the law to join. Some join groups based on their interests, such as sports or even workout programs like CrossFit. There are other opportunities to find communities based around religious beliefs or stages of life—new parents, working moms, and the like. Some communities come together based on social impact, like those that work toward encouraging economic impact in certain sectors. An idea for a small business law firm would be to work with an economic development program to encourage entrepreneurship in their community. Becoming a visible champion of entrepreneurs will help this law firm with visibility, as through service, they are reaching an audience of potential new start-up clients.

For attorneys who are strapped for time, digital communities are another resource for camaraderie and networking. Participation in online or internet communities can involve anything from starting conversations through blog postings to participating in social media groups. Especially for introverts, online communities can be rewarding personally and professionally, allowing them to network on their own terms. Attorneys can seek out business development opportunities online through learning communities, membership communities, newsgroups, and also message boards. Networking through virtual communities can work for B2B and B2C practitioners with the level of access and interaction within the group completely determined by the attorney.

GOOD THINKING

Attorneys interested in participating in digital business development through virtual community activity can begin with a review of the offerings through the American Bar Association. The ABA offers a variety of communities that allow for local and national networking with attorneys in a variety of practice areas such as construction law and communications law. These online circles allow you to connect with practitioners for referrals, education, and camaraderie. The communities have different methods of relationship building such as online forums for discussions and questions, as well as training and CLE sessions. Some even offer large annual conferences that provide a solo and small law firm the opportunity to connect in person with the professionals that they have forged connections with online.

Finding an organization and membership are the first steps in joining a new circle. But enrolling yourself in an organization, adding it to your bio, and calling it good for the next year isn't enough. These are small but necessary preliminary actions, with consistent activity and shared interest being the keys to long-term growth for your practice. Remember, effort and shared interest are essential in the new communities you join. You must show up and contribute to developing your name and brand. People will remember you (and your law practice) through a history of your respectful interactions that include listening, encouragement, and offers for guidance.

HOW TO FIND A COMMUNITY FOR YOUR LAW PRACTICE

The community for your law practice should involve the business or general community, depending on your practice area. It is smart to include legal industry communities in the mix, too. It is not one or the other; it is both. This blended presence of attorneys and non-attorneys in your network is an important ratio to maintain, as it is an easy way to keep referrals and chatter about your practice coming in from different sources.

What is helpful is that finding circles for your practice isn't too hard when you start with what you share in common with others. Lawyers looking to do more in their communities or find communities to be involved with can look to their personal brand or law firm mission statement to determine where to begin. Directionless networking is a time drain, so finding the commonalities between you and the audience you are looking to engage with, whether that be clients or referral sources, will help determine what type of organizations, boards, and groups to join. It is amazing how shared passions create fast friends and colleagues. It is also true that shared experiences like volunteering or event participation with those people can have the same magic.

B2C SPOTLIGHT: FINDING COMMUNITY THROUGH COMMONALITY

A small trusts and estates practice wants to have a larger impact in its community. It starts the process by brainstorming what it has in common with its members. For example, if the lawyers in the law firm are new parents, they might start mapping out their own concerns for their kids. They then match those issues up with their legal services to determine a clear message to the people they look to represent through their trusts and estates practice who are also figuring out what it means to be new parents. Knowing in advance what the attorney has in common with their audience will feed into their marketing (what messaging goes on the website) and also their business development (what groups to join and what to say in those groups).

These trusts and estate attorneys who are also new parents can seek out communities for growing families and come prepared with connection points with this audience. The law firm can expand its presence by determining if its local bar association has a meet-up for new parents that they can join as well. This mixture of circles is ideal for their practice, as they are in front of both potential clients and referral sources.

By networking in the community of new parents that they are most vested in, as it represents their own stage of life, the lawyers keep their interest high. By doing their homework in advance and being certain about what their concerns are when it comes to the future of their own children, they are armed with the networking tidbits necessary for lead generation through casual conversation.

Joining the wrong communities will waste your time and money, and joining too many communities will spread you too thin and result in the same waste of your effort. There is not a formula for exactly how many professional organizations to join, and there isn't an exact mix of legal industry organizations that broaden your visibility and capture more referrals to your practice. Likewise, there isn't necessarily a perfect number of non-lawyer professional organizations to join that will encourage more new clients.

With intention, you can stack the deck in your favor through an understanding of what your goals are for joining a community and then ensuring that their offerings back up those ambitions. The best answer to the question of how many professional communities to join will be unique to you and your law practice. It will be based on your practice goals and balanced by your financial and time budgets. You should anticipate experimenting with new groups or new legal issues that your practice can focus on until you find your right mix.

B2B AND B2C SPOTLIGHT: CHOOSING THE RIGHT CIRCLES

Attorneys who practice in the same space can have entirely different offerings. This example focuses on two healthcare attorneys who need to reach fundamentally different markets to support the goals of their law practices. Although they are both healthcare lawyers, they practice in distinct B2B and B2C areas. In this example, each attorney must tailor their community presence to the legal needs of the healthcare industry they serve.

A B2B healthcare attorney focused on the business side of medicine should be involved in professional circles that include physicians and other medical professionals. This can come through membership in medical societies or other groups that promote health-related causes and support medical professionals. This attorney should also be involved in bar association activities locally and nationally, with specific attention paid to membership in sections that support their law practice. A good example would be engaging in both the healthcare and business law sections of their bar association to cross-promote and capture more visibility with potential co-counsel and referral sources.

A B2C healthcare attorney who focuses on the issues that can affect a medical professional regarding federal criminal charges or licensure defense will have different communities to network with. This attorney should have a consistent presence and promotion within the medical community. They might speak at high-level doctor-attended conferences related to personal risk and liability. This attorney's law firm could use its blog to promote thought leadership on issues that lead to healthcare fraud charges, such as coding or kickbacks. This B2C attorney should also network with other attorneys, including the healthcare and business law sections of their bar associations, and should also add general criminal defense practitioners into the mix. These criminal law attorneys might not specialize in the nuanced practice of healthcare defense at the federal level, leading to attorney-to-attorney referrals coming into the practice.

HOW TO VET YOUR OPPORTUNITIES

You have many avenues to vet the communities you join to ensure that they are a good fit for you and your business development goals. Reviewing an organization's resources and activities is part of the vetting process, but being honest about your commitment to involvement is the real challenge. When you are considering joining a new organization, being engaged will be key. There is no point in joining an organization that you are not passionate about or involved with. These types of passive memberships flesh out your CV but ultimately will have no impact on your ability to bring business into the law firm. So, the act of joining a professional community isn't the end goal—the end goal is activity, visibility, and true participation.

Consider these areas to help you determine if a community organization, in the legal community or not, is a good fit for your practice.

Reach

It is vital to know what part of your audience or community the organization is involved in. By the time you are interested in extending your visibility through business development in professional organizations, you should have a concrete understanding of your audience. You will need to determine how the organization fits into your plans. This will be different for everyone, as some attorneys use professional organizational activities for outreach, education, and visibility. Knowing in advance what the opportunities are to connect directly with your target audience is important. Being a member of an organization should provide you with a list of active ways to be in touch with its members, such as large followings on their social media channels, consistent webinars or educational activities, or newsletters with demonstrated open rates that you can contribute to.

Review

When vetting a community, research the organization a bit. You will want to review its website and its history. There might be an area on an organization's website where you learn about its mission and goals. Be sure to check out the biographies of key staff members and learn about their board. Review the people associated with the organization as carefully as you review the organization itself, as there could be opportunities for business development once relationships are established. Be sure to pay attention to the size of the organization, as it is easier to create business development connections in the local chapter of a large organization or in a hyper-local group of professionals that serves the same population of people in your general area.

Activities

The organization's online presence can give you a taste of its social calendar. Determine if there are opportunities for your law practice through volunteering and local events. Be sure to take notes, as you might find opportunities to be of service. For example, maybe your law practice can fill a hole in the organization's calendar by creating your own educational event that will support its mission and its audience as well as your business development goals. You will want to pay attention to areas related to visibility, such as guest posting on their blog, participation in their events through sponsorship, and even the cadence of their get-togethers. If they meet for happy hour every Tuesday, it sounds awesome, but can you honestly make that consistently happen? Additionally, organizational membership also helps you attain skills or prospects that you don't otherwise have. A lawyer looking to know more decision-makers in an industry might spearhead a project that gives them face time with their dream audience. Likewise, an attorney who wants to develop their skills in public speaking might cut their teeth on short presentations to just the board of the organization to gain experience.

Service

Pay attention to their existing service and volunteer programs and take note of what you can join. Lawyers have an elevated status in our society as professionals directly linked to fundamental principles of justice, safety, and fairness. The way our community regards attorneys comes with immense privilege. It is important to leverage that privilege to help others in the community. You can do this through education, such as legal nights, or through introductions to people in your network who can fast-track a project or issue that your community is struggling with.

Reputation

Make time to review the feedback on this organization. What are other people saying? A lot of this information is public and can be seen in online reviews. A reputation check can also happen through conversations in your network seeking out opinions from other professionals like legal practitioners on what their experience has been to ensure membership will be a good use of your efforts.

Think Critically

Vetting the organization is vital to ensuring that it is a good fit for you and your law firm. In most cases, professional organizations and nonprofits are friendly toward attorneys joining them, especially if they intend to contribute and participate in a shared mission. But their interest in you is not enough. Don't rely on a great first impression with an organization or only your friend's advice when it comes to determining where to spend your business development efforts; be smart and strategic. Use the following evaluative questions to guide you in determining the suitability of organizations for your business development.

- How does this organization fit with the goals you have set for business development?
- How does this organization put you in front of your target audience and/or referral sources?
- What types of opportunities to serve are available through the organization?
- How expensive is the membership?
- How saturated is the organization with other attorneys or law firms?
- What is the time commitment to truly participate in the organization?
- Are there pathways to leadership?

Know Your Power

You will want to know in advance how being involved in this organization will address your business development goals and how you can combine them with your ability to serve the community. This type of strategic planning can be fleshed out in an initial meeting with the organization's key players. Don't feel nervous requesting this introductory meeting with them; it is in accordance with someone who is serious about vetting an organization for long-term participation and sends a message that you are aware of your value.

If you do ask for a meeting with the organization during the vetting stage, come prepared. You are interviewing them as much as they are interviewing you. Lawyers bring tremendous value to organizations through their volunteer work. Most organizations know that attorneys make great members, especially board members, as they are trained to see risk differently than other professionals. Having a lawyer as a member opens the doors to recruiting other attorneys to their organizations, as lawyers have skill sets such as risk management that stand out from other professionals.

So, before your meeting, sketch out your plan. Make the most of your time so you walk away from your meeting with answers to big questions like what their one-year goals are and how they compare to the greater strategic five-year goals of the organization or its mission. Your plan should include questions about the weekly or monthly responsibilities associated with being a member of their organization and an understanding of exactly what their offerings are for your career and the community you serve. You can also seek to learn about the success stories of other professionals who have joined this organization as a member and what part the organization played in their career trajectory.

ENGAGEMENT WITH THE COMMUNITY

It is important to recognize your place and your role when joining any established community or organization, especially if the end goal is business development. You might be the only lawyer in a community that you join, and that is an opportunity to show leadership in addition to showcasing your personal brand.

When joining a new community, press pause and take note of your surroundings. There are many landmines in all circles, even professional ones. Attorneys need to be aware of common misconceptions about them or about their community to navigate issues as they come up. They also need to be aware of sensitive matters in a community that have negative strings attached to them and should be actively avoided. When wading into the water of a new community, start slowly. Look for ways to contribute and to help in a respectful manner with a supportive attitude. If your goal is long-term connection, it is important to adapt to the new community you are in by getting to know the people and the issues. The mindset shouldn't be focused on fixing anyone but rather on contributing help through your legal services, your legal education, or just your presence as a devoted professional community member.

Engagement with a new community will start with introducing yourself, and then that introduction gains memorability through the momentum of consistent activity. Showing interest in the community by attending events, joining committees, and having positive, consistent interactions with members will help your business development efforts take a shape. Be sure to add your community events and organizational meetings to your calendar in advance so you can plan around them.

Lawyers can also promote interaction between members of the group by initiating lunches and coffees or even hosting events at their firm. Many attorneys join communities with the goal of eventually taking on a more formal leadership role, so they look for ways to meaningfully contribute along the way. These contributions have a great effect on increasing visibility and confirming your shared values, passions, or goals.

From the perspective of learning, you might request site visits for new projects the organization is working on or invite a few of the board members for a walking tour of the neighborhood that they serve. Learning about the community and the audience that an organization serves will enhance your understanding of the needs and how you can help through your legal services.

Seeing an organization's inner workings and how it meets the needs of the population it serves, including meeting the staff—basically, the people who keep the train moving every day—will influence your perception of the laws that affect it and the challenges it faces. Engaging with a new community is a great opportunity for business development in addition to professional growth.

INCLUDING INCLUSION

Inclusion helps foster respect in a community. It allows for a safe space for its members to participate and feel valued. Joining a new community can be a dance with issues to navigate, avoid, or challenge. It is important to be aware of the perceptions that you are walking into so that you can be the first lawyer they meet who is totally different, in an amazing way, from what they expected.

How does the community perceive attorneys? Some communities, especially minority and marginalized groups, struggle to see themselves as a valued part of the justice system. Growing up, they might have seen the justice system as a wall of negativity formed through a blend of interactions with police, district attorneys, and judges.

For others, they might have had a bad interaction with an attorney who was supposed to be on their side.

A cursory search on Google with the phrase "Why is my lawyer ___" triggers a list of previous searches made by someone's previous clients.

- Why is my lawyer *mad at me*?
- Why is my lawyer *not calling me*?
- Why is my lawyer *ignoring me*?
- Why is my lawyer *yelling at me*?

Through Google's honest algorithmic results, we understand that many legal practitioners have set the bar low for positive interactions between lawyers and clients as well as community members.

Joining a new circle is an opportunity for you to be intentionally different. An easy way to have a more inclusive perspective when joining a new organization is to check your arrogance at the door.

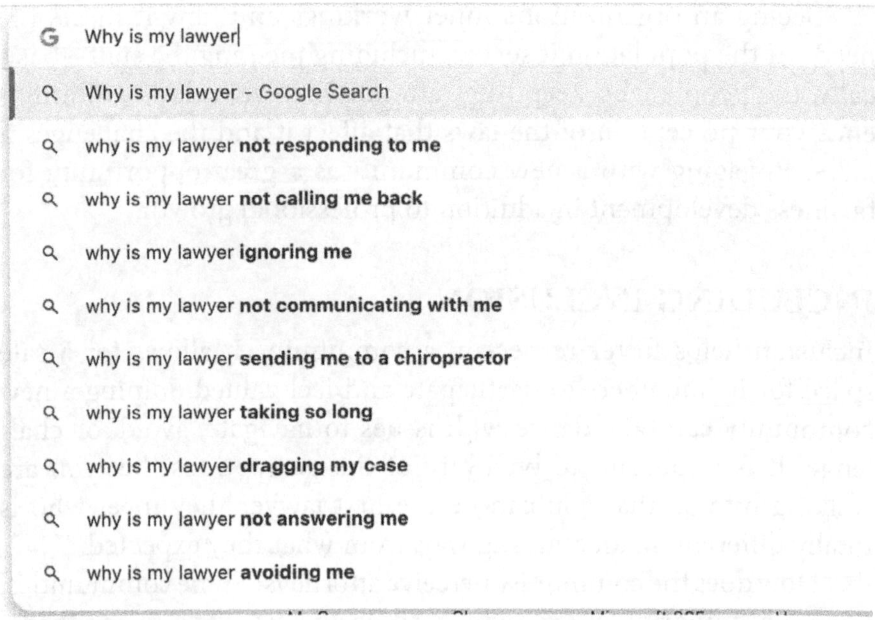

Figure 3.1 Sample of Google's Autocomplete Prediction (Image by Author)

You can be risk-averse without being a negative wet blanket. One Harvard Business Review article shared, "humility *in the service of ambition* is the most effective and sustainable mindset for leaders who aspire to do big things[.]"[3] It is true—you can be knowledgeable without being smug and rude. It is a balance but one everyone can master.

Additionally, pay attention to issues that require sensitivity and engage with grace. Freedom of expression is different in communities within and outside the law, which can lead to sticky situations. You will want to figure out your group's norms so everyone, including you, is clear on what is appropriate. Remember that one bad interaction with you can unravel years of a hard-earned reputation

[3] https://hbr.org/2018/10/if-humility-is-so-important-why-are-leaders-so-arrogant.

in a community. People talk, and when you are considerate of your audience and their challenges, you are more likely to give them something good to say about you and your law firm.

INVESTING IN YOUR COMMUNITY

As part of a community organization, you are part of its culture. Lawyers can lead the charge in a community by using their energy and network as much as their voice. Investing in your community includes starting inclusive conversations and making positive connections between people you respect who don't know each other yet. Chances are you have colleagues you can connect with the group or might be able to cross-promote with group members. Depending on the community you are joining, there will be opportunities to spread awareness in different ways. By participating in an educational campaign or just consistently committing to public commentary (even if it is limited to social media profiles) on why the organization matters to you, you invest in your community. You also can start to establish yourself as an ambassador. If the public learns from you or sees you involved in awareness activities, they are more likely to trust your law firm and your legal services.

Being a true part of a community does include the thoughtful donation of your time. For some, this might look like attendance at a community's charity event, and for others, it might be the entire administration of the charity event. Estate planning lawyers might volunteer their time in the community in a branded way by doing pro bono work at a senior center, whereas a small business law firm with a niche in the corporate side of environmental law might spend time planting trees in their community. Attorneys can host recycling days at their offices where community members can drop off electronics or batteries. Law firms can likewise offer notary services for free or at a discounted price in their neighborhoods. These examples illustrate ways that community membership is more than prompt payment of your professional dues. It takes work to show up for others, and that work can be rewarded through an elevated status in your community along with referrals to your law practice.

GOOD THINKING

With over 1.3 million attorneys practicing in this country, can you imagine the good that would happen in our communities if all licensed lawyers contributed 50 hours of pro bono time per year to those who are disadvantaged? Solo and small law firms looking to do more in their communities should consider the following ideas for pro bono work:

- *A Gallup poll found that "slightly less than half of U.S. adults, 46%, have a will that describes how they would like their money and estate to be handled after their death."[4] Small law firm lawyers could provide discounted services related to will preparation for certain populations.*
- *A survey found that "[m]any Americans do not know what rights are protected under the First Amendment and a substantial number cannot name all three branches of government."[5] Solo practice lawyers can add an educational component to their online presence to teach their communities about constitutionally protected rights.*
- *Depending on their industry, businesses spend 2%–20% of their gross revenue on commercial property rent.[6] Attorneys can provide guidance during the leasing process for small business owners, as well as information regarding leasing options and amendments, and prevent disputes.*

---

[4] https://news.gallup.com/poll/351500/how-many-americans-have-will.aspx#:~:-text=WASHINGTON%2C%20D.C.%20%2D%2D%20Gallup's%20latest,on%20this%20question%20since%201990.

[5] https://www.governing.com/government-quotes/it-is-worrisome-that-one-in-six-u-s-adults-cannot-name-any-of-the-branches-of-government.

[6] https://commercialonebrokers.com/percentage-of-business-income-spent-on-rent/.

> - ***The Federal Trade Commission is addressing the issue of noncompete agreements and published, "An estimated 30 million workers—nearly one in five Americans—are subject to a noncompete."[7] Solo and small firm lawyers who work with either employees on the plaintiff side or employers on the business side of noncompete agreements have a lot of high-level insight to offer their respective communities.***

CONVERSATIONS IN THE COMMUNITY

When you join a new community, you will want to ensure that your brand and business development goals are at the forefront of your mind. Solo and small law firm attorneys are usually on their own when it comes to preparing what they will say and do at professional events. You can set yourself up for success by developing a few bullet points to prompt your business development mindset and assist with conversations.

#1: The Pregame

Reminding yourself exactly how you help people or companies for a living through your great legal services will change how you enter a room. It will also change the memorability of your law practice and ensure you put your best foot forward in networking situations, which will always have a positive effect on the return.

The pregame for networking is easier than you think. It is smart to keep a short list of your law firm's greatest qualities or initiatives and the ways your legal services are distinct. If you are creative and solution-oriented, be sure to have a few examples handy to share that will resonate with the audience you will be involved with.

If it is your first or fifth time going to a professional event, it is vital to know who you are meeting and what matters to them.

---

[7] https://www.ftc.gov/news-events/news/press-releases/2024/04/ftc-announces-rule-banning-noncompetes.

A cursory review of the headlines prior to networking events through the lens of the issues you solve through your law practice goes a long way. Topical information can also be found on the website of the event host or the websites of the major sponsors. Normally, the leadership of any organization can be found on their website, making it easy to learn a bit about the background of the major players.

Preparing for your success when it comes to networking helps you become a strong match with your audience. Looking for connections between your law practice and other people's interests in news headlines, on websites, and in biography descriptions takes work, but the result is authentic connections and more effective business development.

Changing your business development focus from "What's in it for me?" to "How I serve others" takes intention. However, better business development comes from a collaborative and helpful mindset based on how you help others and how your legal services solve their challenges.

B2B SPOTLIGHT: WHITE-COLLAR DEFENSE PRACTICE

A white-collar defense attorney looking forward to attending a large professional conference of CPAs prepares beforehand in a few smart ways through the following activities:

- Proactively scanning the headlines before the event, the attorney looks for trends in professional accounting or items of interest, ensuring they are well informed and ready for industry-centered discussion.
- Generally reviewing the most common white-collar prosecutions that year, the attorney gains a comprehensive understanding of the issues from the perspective of professional accountancy.

- Noting a few preventable or topical issues that led to white-collar investigations or charges and how those issues relate to their legal services.
- Reviewing their website biography and ensuring it was updated and reflects the reputation and results of their law practice.
- Practicing their elevator pitch and adding proactive insights into how CPAs can play a big role in white-collar defense cases through an introduction to a skilled attorney.

With these steps, this white-collar defense attorney is preparing for networking success in a professional circle outside the legal industry. The attorney's clear objective at this conference is to establish new CPA contacts for potential client referrals. This focus helps them concentrate on what matters to the audience they will be in front of. The attorney is ready with conversation starters and ideas to ask insightful questions, building authentic connections with the accounting professionals at the conference.

If you go into a networking event committed to making the most of your time there and securing the best results possible, it shows. Preparing and even hyping yourself up before going to events affects your energy and ensures fluidity in what you say about your law practice. This confidence is key to having better conversations in different communities where you can promote your services. You win when you prepare, and no one knows that better than attorneys.

#2: The Elevator Pitch

There is nothing worse than hearing a rambling answer to the question "And what do you do for a living?" or even the shortest answer possible that contains zero business development information or room for follow-up, "I am a lawyer." Networking in any professional capacity requires you to introduce yourself repeatedly. These introductions can make or break how you are received by a new contact or community. Elevator pitches are succinct and prepared introductions about your law practice, and regardless of the type of law you practice, you need at least one.

With an elevator pitch in your back pocket, you will always have something polished to say should you encounter a potential client or referral source in pretty much any situation. These prepared statements not only give an organic-feeling first impression of who you are and who you help and serve, but they also help you stand out in a crowded networking event. They allow you to quickly and effectively communicate your value proposition, making it easier for others to remember you and your services. It isn't a stretch to say that professionals are busy people (in and out of the legal industry). Things move quickly at networking events, and our collective shrinking attention span doesn't help when it comes to being memorable to new people. Elevator pitches are meant for this brevity.

GOOD THINKING

The origin story of the "elevator pitch" is murky, with a few different people claiming credit. These short statements are not just a formality, but a crucial tool in law firm business development and personal marketing. They serve as your introduction, answering the question "Why do you matter to me?" in a way that is both engaging and informative.

Elevator pitches—concise 30-second statements, about 75 words, about how you help through your legal services—are not just introductions. They are strategic tools that begin with the same base or root statement and are tweaked depending on who you are talking to. Clients need to hear something different than referral sources, and lawyers looking to get more from their business development know how to introduce themselves in a noteworthy way on the fly.

When developing your elevator pitch, remember that the point is connection. It will be tempting to say what matters to you, but adjusting the way you introduce yourself *to address what matters to them* works better. Elevator pitches are short, and those 30 seconds are wasted quickly if you don't have at least an idea of who you are meeting and what matters to them. Coming up with a first sentence that is personal or career-centered works well to relay who you are and what your law firm does for others.

It is helpful to write out your elevator pitch so you can note the length and cadence while you practice it. It will seem so smooth in your head, but even the most seasoned attorney stumbles the first few times when saying their elevator pitch out loud before it feels natural. You will feel weird while doing it, but trying out your elevator pitch in front of a mirror or even in the privacy of your car a few times before you enter the event will help calm nerves and make you more prepared.

Consider the sample elevator pitches that follow.

B2B ELEVATOR PITCH TO A POTENTIAL CLIENT

I'm John Charles, a business lawyer with Charles Law Partners. We focus on legal services for Colorado companies and help our small business clients, like yourself, reduce stress by optimizing their contracts, operations, and tax liabilities. It would be great to learn more about your team. Where are your operations based?

In this B2B example, a clear connection is made between what the lawyer does for a living and how that matters to the small business audience. This short overview is loaded with helpful information for the intended audience to connect with. They have mentioned their local focus on Colorado small businesses while weaving in aspects of the operational issues that burden many small businesspeople, such as taxes and operational challenges. They have made a very clear association between their legal services being a potential new solution to existing problems. There is even a connection to the stress that businesspeople feel, an oftentimes invisible but very much real emotional component of running a corporation of any size.

B2C ELEVATOR PITCH TO A REFERRAL SOURCE

I'm John Charles, a family law attorney with Charles Law Partners. For 20 years, my solo law firm has served the same folks you do: families in our local community that are in transition and facing divorce or custody issues. I would love to learn more about your family therapy practice. How long have you been in business?

This B2C elevator pitch example packs in a ton of information meant to connect directly with the intended audience, a referral source. They were able to qualify their experience in length and make a direct link to the therapist's niche. The pitch succinctly shares what type of family law issues they solve and connects the firm to the local community.

#3: Downtime, Small Talk, and Awkward Moments

The professional world, including the legal industry, is rife with networking opportunities, and these necessarily include downtime, small talk, and other socially awkward moments. Planning is the easiest and most effective strategy to keep a conversation going. If you know who you are in front of and, at least, have a general strategy related to the point of you being at the same event and how that relates back to your law practice, you should be in good shape. Social events are opportunities to learn more about others who might need your legal services or can refer them to others.

In social situations where you are looking to connect with new people, listen more than you speak. Open-ended questions backed up by some preparation regarding the people or the issues that you all care about or the industry that you both serve can make small talk more natural. If you have reviewed some information about the event you are attending or current topics or issues affecting that industry, it is easy to talk through what would otherwise be downtime in networking or a lull in conversation.

In these moments of weirdness, when it would be easier to pull out your phone or only talk to the people you already know, remind yourself of the opportunities to connect you are missing out on. Remember, you are at this event for a reason; often, you have paid in some way through membership or admission to be there, so make the most of it. Prepare in advance for the inevitable downtime and moments for small talk with a plan of pivoting conversations from topics or even pivoting away from people.

Awkwardness comes in all shapes and sizes in professional networking. For some, it can mean forgetting the name of someone super important in the community. For others, it can mean an unavoidable interaction with someone in your community who you truly dislike or who owes you money. Or even worse, a weird conversation followed by dead silence. Silence is calming in many situations, but professional networking events are not one of them.

Uncomfortable situations put you off. They change your mood, depending on gravity, and they might even make you feel visibly emotional. We are human, and some of this is inevitable. It helps to control what you can in that moment—if that is your heart racing, insert the breathing techniques you learned in yoga class years ago and turn your focus elsewhere for a few minutes. If the most obnoxious person you have ever met in a professional capacity is seated at the same table with you at the event, take the high road, make eye contact, and genuinely ask them how their world is, what is new, and what is going on.

There is nothing gained by avoiding great networking opportunities because of the threat of dealing with uncomfortable situations. In my experience, these moments never stop altogether, and everyone experiences them at some point in their professional career. But each time you meet the challenge of awkward moments with preparation, you get better at controlling your reaction. You add tools to your toolbox that help you act more naturally on the outside than you might feel on the inside.

#4: Following Up

The follow-up after the event is just as important as attending. Common goals for professional socializing include broadening your network to meet new people or developing a deeper insight into an industry. Being clear about what your networking goals are when attending professional events helps define your follow-up strategy. For example, if you are looking to meet new referral sources, you will want to focus on collecting contact information through business cards or on LinkedIn so you can stay connected. You might add the same contact information to your law firm's email campaign into a segmented email list for professional referral sources where they will receive messaging throughout the year. The follow-up messaging should be consistent to confirm how you help and serve the same community and how your client services align with theirs, with a clear takeaway message that your law firm is a great option for service.

GOOD THINKING

LinkedIn is a top choice for solo and small firm networking and follow-up. An ABA survey found that LinkedIn is the leading platform at 76 percent, followed by Facebook (60 percent), Twitter (37 percent), Martindale (35 percent), and Avvo (22 percent).[8] Attorneys can effectively implement a robust follow-up strategy using a basic or free LinkedIn account. The platform's basic account offerings allow lawyers to connect with new colleagues, request and provide recommendations regarding their legal services, and search and review profiles of other LinkedIn members. With a regular posting schedule, attorneys can confirm their brand and offerings, making LinkedIn a great, and economical, choice for networking and follow-up needs.

---

[8] https://www.americanbar.org/groups/law_practice/resources/legal-technology-resource-center/tech-survey/2020/.

What is great about follow-up for solo and small law firms is that everyone gets to choose their channels. Depending on the amount of time and money that you want to spend, your post-event follow-up strategy can mirror that of larger law firms. There are tons of options when it comes to software that will help you send targeted texts and emails with the push of a button. Other firms have a few blog posts on their website that are "evergreen" and are always relevant to the issue or industry you are trying to speak to long after they have been published. Evergreen content can be sent as a follow-up through email to a new contact or prospective client, with a quick email message that confirms it was great to meet them and here is a blog post that speaks directly to some of the items you spoke about. The follow-up plan can include an offer to meet the person for lunch later in the month or even to speak by phone when they have time.

Being in a solo or small law firm means that you will probably be the one to map out a follow-up plan that connects directly with your professional networking goals. Your plan for implementing follow-up will also reflect your brand and personal preferences regarding marketing channels. So, if you hate LinkedIn, don't plan to use it; the efforts will fall flat because the necessary interest to make it worthwhile is not there. It is more effective to find a few ways that work well for you when it comes to follow-up after networking; stick to them and repeat them consistently, and they will become an extension of your brand.

In smaller law firms, you can customize a lot of what you do when it comes to follow-up. Sending a new contact a few articles by email related to your previous discussion is a great idea to continue a conversation. Likewise, a handwritten note received in the mail after an initial contact looks and feels classy in an increasingly digital world. Not everyone will follow up in the same way, so if you prefer to use email, text, LinkedIn, handwritten notes, or all of the above, do so. Personal touches matter when you are trying to make a true connection, and in a smaller law firm, your follow-up can be distinct to you.

The end goal of follow-up is to stay in contact with the people you meet when networking so your law practice can see a return on the investment you make by attending events in the community. Tracking your activities will determine whether you are treading water or moving forward with your goals. Some small firms use online Customer Relationship Management systems, also known as CRMs.[9] These are cloud-based software options for tracking your relationships or leads. CRMs manage how you stay connected with your potential clients and referral sources by tracking the communications you are involved in with each individual or group, including the number and types of interactions coming out of your law firm.

A good use of a CRM for a small law firm would be tracking the contacts their attorneys make throughout the year, prompting follow-up a few times with leads, and then the law firm can show through data how much business has come from the effort, what efforts create more business, and what efforts need to be cut out of the strategy entirely. There are options for CRM systems that connect directly to billing software, providing a more complete financial picture for a smaller law firm. These platforms can reveal how much money the firm earns per month, what it takes to maintain that through existing revenue streams, and the cost to acquire new leads.

Regardless of whether you are using a spreadsheet or a CRM to track your business development results, you will want to save your sanity by being realistic. You will not knock it out of the park at every event, with each leading to a gazillion new connections for your law firm. In the real world, maybe one or two great new introductions through each event mean business development success. Tracking results in business development is also not black and white, as results of relationship building can take longer to take shape, sometimes

---

[9] Salesforce defines a CRM as "a tool used for contact management, sales management, agent productivity, and more. The goal of a CRM system is simple: Improve business relationships to grow your business. CRM tools help you manage customer relationships across the entire customer lifecycle, at every marketing, sales, e-commerce, and customer service interaction."

even years. Know in advance that your results of business development might not be immediately visible or tangible, and that is why the follow-up plan is so imperative to ensure a return.

INCLUDING INCLUSION

Your circles can reflect the different types of people in our community. In the legal industry, there will be various options to choose from when it comes to joining bar associations. The easy button will be to join the largest organizations around. When you are in this vetting stage, consider widening your lens to review the offerings of the smaller bar associations that can open doors for your practice. Smaller organizations serving attorneys in a specific county or lawyers with a minority or ethnic background provide excellent opportunities for camaraderie, business development, and networking.

You don't have to be a particular culture or community member to join a specialty bar association. Membership in a specialty bar association is a form of allyship that directly increases your cultural awareness and viewpoint regarding empathy for others. Experiencing communities outside your own also helps you understand your brand better. These experiences make us more relatable to others. Smaller and specialty bar associations will have great opportunities to contribute, grow, and learn.

REAL-WORLD ETHICS

Attorneys running their own business development and marketing strategies know that marketing technology is moving faster than the ethical rules can keep up. Attorneys looking into joining new and different circles to reach people in specific communities and professional organizations might be tempted to cut corners in long-term business development through faster tactics. *Attorneys should consider the rules of each state they are licensed to practice in as well as their personal ethics when making marketing decisions.*

Geotargeting is a great example of a digital marketing option that many B2B and B2C law practices are presented with. Wikipedia defines this type of online marketing as a "method of delivering different content to visitors based on their geolocation."[10] Chances are you have personally experienced geotargeting, as this is the marketing that puts personalized content on your phone that feels like it was made for you; it sees and understands you. This is the content that follows you to every website and app you use. Through geotargeting, you can use a person's location to send them content at the exact moment when they are most likely to convert to a client. As geotargeting can exclude audiences as much as it can include them, it makes attorney marketing more potent in reaching the intended audience. But again, geotargeting an audience through a food delivery app is very different from geotargeting a person recovering in the hospital. In considering what type of lawyer you are and what kind of law firm you will run, navigating grey areas is where personal and professional ethics will affect your marketing.

***

Creating a professional network that reflects your law practice goals takes effort. The organizations or nonprofits that you commit to are your circle. To become an attorney in a community that occupies a defined space and is "*the person* to talk to" takes effort. There are many different opportunities to join communities that align with your law practice and its goals. But seeing networking events as a drag on your time or even "forced fun" will absolutely overshadow your results. If you are taking the time to join a new community, in the law or outside, be open.

There will be new people to introduce your practice to, so be ready to walk through that door when it opens. There will be opportunities to train and educate, and those might be better options for you if you cannot stand the idea of "schmoozing." Additionally, boards and committees can provide occasions to distinguish your law practice through service. You will need to reach back as much as you are reaching forward—being open can be exhibited through

[10] https://en.wikipedia.org/wiki/Geotargeting.

a willingness to introduce people to others in your network when you know they could be served well by that connection. But if you want to avoid the trap of joining a new community, paying the dues, attending the events, and getting to the end of the year and thinking, "That was all for nothing," remember that this aspect of your business development strategy is held up by your preparation and follow-up.

4

Cultivate

> ***Leadership is an action, not a position.***
>
> **—Donald McGannon**

Becoming a great leader is a career-long quest. This chapter discussion focuses on the leadership growth required in business development. Solo and small law firm attorneys are given an understanding of how leadership positions credential a legal career and provide insight into how to follow a branded leadership path for business development. The information in this chapter supports attorneys who want to learn more about having a more significant impact or legacy in their careers through leadership roles.

***

There is a passive gain in professional growth that happens for everyone. Over the years, you improve at everything from big to small, including practicing law and business development as well as introducing yourself and networking. The superstars in the solo and small law firm world view professional growth intentionally and include leadership as much as they can in their career paths.

In business development, your personal growth and the leadership opportunities that you pursue are entirely in your control. Lawyers who are leaders can move mountains, and some do. They know that with intention and commitment, anything is possible. This is contrasted by lawyers who lead on a smaller scale. They aren't looking to head an entire organization, effort, or cause. They find leadership opportunities in smaller acts that back up their brands, such as leading a committee or being a board member of a section of an organization. Both versions of leadership are admirable and reflect the lawyers' strengths.

As there are an unlimited number of ways that attorneys can become leaders in the community or show leadership in their law practices, it is key to have a clear vision of what you intend leadership roles will do for your reputation and your business development. It is possible to show leadership in your career through a history of mentorship and the long-term influence you have had on the next generation of attorneys. Leadership on a micro level, through one-on-one relationships like mentoring, can be easier to manage from a time standpoint and be a better fit for people who have introverted personalities. Mentoring someone tells a story of your respect for others, an industry, or a profession. It also showcases your qualifications as a leader in the community by being a role model.

This is juxtaposed by macro leadership roles, such as running a state or national bar association by serving as a president. Serving as a president of a bar association is a credential that is instantly recognizable outside the law. It is a long-lasting aspect of your career legacy, as it shows a clear alignment with the organization's principles and beliefs, which usually touch on qualities of integrity and credibility. However, serving as the president of a bar association is a difficult task that can be a multi-year commitment, depending on the organization's setup. It can be a demanding position for a small law firm owner given the number of hats they already wear.

For small law firms, the best way to ensure long-term success in leadership roles and positions is to stay visible. For small firm attorneys, that doesn't necessarily mean writing big checks, so your law firm's logo is displayed at every event. Visibility comes in all shapes and sizes and figuring out how to consistently affirm your brand through leadership and then promoting causes you care about through a plan works well. This can include sharing information about a movement, a plight, or a community you are dedicated to on your social media pages. Being a mentor to someone matters, and especially as a small law firm attorney, you should get credit for that; an idea would be to capture the success of your mentor/mentee experience in an article written for your law school's alumni publication. Likewise, serving on boards or leading committees tells the world about the investment you have in your community. A small firm can request to add the logos of organizations they are involved with to their website to earn a little extra marketing mileage from the effort. Community activity through leadership positions affirms your brand and its meaning to others and directly impacts your targeted business development. Visibility helps your business development by making your good deeds known. As your status and influence grow, the need to be intentional about cultivating leadership in your career becomes more imperative. Leadership and professional development benefit your law firm as a business as well. When you expand to a new level, you take your firm with you.

WHAT IS LEADERSHIP IN THE SOLO AND SMALL FIRM WORLD?

When we hear leadership in the legal profession, the larger-than-life lawyer who is also an amazing public speaker who runs a huge bar association while balancing a successful law practice and holding a prominent position on a paid corporate board might come to mind. But there is no archetypal situation when it comes to lawyers in leadership. They don't look the same, act the same, or have the same results. There is no cookie-cutter approach to cultivating leadership in your career or for your small law firm.

Put very simply, attorneys who lead in their professional lives support their personal goals by helping others. True leadership is found in a person's actions as much as it is found in their words. Indeed, lawyers who lead are careful about what they say because their words must be backed up by complementary actions and activities. There will never be a standard definition of leadership for everyone because it reflects the impact you would like your practice to have on an audience or an issue combined with the effort you can exhibit, including the time and energy you can expend. Even with the definition of leadership being a moving target, you know it when you see it.

Big Leadership in a Small Law Firm

The opportunities for leadership in the professional world come in all shapes and sizes. They can include work with individuals in a community, as well as with organizations and associations. Small law firm leaders can direct a group of people toward achieving their collective vision faster or in a more risk-averse manner. They can also engage in smaller acts of leadership that can often wield more considerable influence, such as career mentorship and sponsorship. The difference between mentorship and sponsorship of others is that "[a] mentor is a person who gives a protégé advice, answers questions, strategizes career moves and professional development. A sponsor is someone who promotes a protégé to other people to help advance the protégé's career. A pithy way to remember the distinction is this: 'Mentors talk to you. Sponsors talk *about* you to powerful people when you aren't in the room.'" Mentors guide through conversations. Sponsors advocate more actively and serve as champions for career advancement through their influence on others.

The lawyers who are leaders might be afraid to take personal risks by stepping into the spotlight but do it anyway. They know that they will not develop or grow if they are stagnant in their law practice and business development. They expect new and different results because they are constantly challenging themselves. They make calculated gambles within their practice areas or niches that push them outside their comfort zones.

Consider the following examples of leadership on small and large scales. They are different in the way that they are executed but similar in the way that they shine a light on the lawyer's leadership:

- A small law firm attorney consistently publicly praises others on LinkedIn as it boosts motivation and reinforces positive

behaviors in others. They treat people in this manner always, inside and outside their law firm.
- A male solo practitioner who volunteers a few times a month through activities hosted by the local women's bar association. When they volunteer, they are collaborative and accountable and actively contribute to the group through active listening and respectful behavior.
- A B2B practitioner on a nonprofit board leads by example, showing up prepared and on time for all meetings. They motivate others on their board by exhibiting their devotion to collaboration, adaptability, and camaraderie at every opportunity.
- A B2C attorney joins the state bar association right out of law school and stays committed to the organization for years. They participate in events, lead committees, and mentor others. This lawyer progresses through the levels of leadership in the bar association intentionally to hold executive positions until they ascend to the president level.
- A business attorney loves the art scene and runs their own solo practice. They rely on their reputation in the business world to network their way onto a prominent board of the city's art museum. This position allows them to personally know the top philanthropists in the state who have the biggest connections in the business community, feeding directly into their business development and networking plans.

Take these ideas as inspiration as the attorneys lead through activism, volunteering, and support of others. Exhibiting leadership is a great way that small and solo firm attorneys can contribute to their communities and to their careers.

The Role of Legacy in Leadership

Lawyers who are leaders in their communities shape their careers for future success. Although it might not be their original intention, they are designing their professional legacies. Holding a position of leadership in a community adds more prestige to your legal career, which reflects well on your law firm.

In general, attorneys hold an elevated reputation in our society as stewards of the justice system and gatekeepers of legal knowledge. This type of occupational privilege is associated with impressive degrees and access to authority that others in the community just don't have. While this occupational privilege is innate to the profession, a legacy of leadership is not. Pursuing a leadership path for your law practice is as much a business decision as it is a personal decision. The right leadership roles exhibit your legal prowess in addition to your trustworthiness, communication skills, and commitment to others. They add to your story and any brand image you are developing for yourself.

Leaders in the legal community draw from the same internal focus and resolve that helped them get through anything hard in life, including law school. This resolve drives them forward and propels them to the top of an industry, a community, or a bar association. These same internal influences play a role in developing successful leadership legacies. They can include personality and personal attributes and can be augmented by environment, including family background and location. It is also true that combining what is personal and unique to you with your professional network can reveal why a leadership role was right for you and not for your colleague with a similar law practice. This decision to go left when your colleague went right will impact your leadership opportunities and your legacy.

The professional legacy of an attorney lives on after they have retired. Legacy reflects impact and some of the best examples we see are buildings named after amazing attorneys in our cities. It can also include being known for having the biggest jury verdicts or securing the most notable clients around. Legacy is derived from positively impacting legal careers through that mentorship and sponsorship or the impact on individuals and families that you have worked with. Lawyers who are educators leave a legacy through community service and the influence they have on the students they teach. Your law practice's legacy shows the tangible difference you have made in the world, and your business development efforts that include leadership roles can craft it with you.

Articulating the legacy you will pursue for your law practice starts with you—who do you want to help and why, or what type of impact do you want to have on society, an organization, or a group of people? A positive legacy in the law is the sum of what you brought to the table during your legal career and how that work made people feel. It reflects the impact your work as an attorney had on the lives of other people. Legacy reflects your service to others and is not tied in any way to the size of the law firm you are with. Leadership and legacy can be a part of a business development strategy for solo and small law firms. Combined, they remind your community of your character and commitment.

QUALITIES NEEDED TO LEAD

The qualities that you develop as a good leader in the community, in the law, and outside the law will make you a better professional and a better person. They will also improve you as a business owner, employer, mentor, and vendor of professional services. Being able to show a history of leadership positions reveals high-level qualities that are positive for your law practice. Qualities such as accountability, integrity, and consistency can feel intangible and difficult to prove but can be gleaned from activities and participation. Leadership roles executed properly *show* your audience who you are rather than just telling them.

Leadership roles, paid or not, expand your career journey. They allow you to develop as a person, and the qualities associated with leadership will reflect positively on your law firm. Leadership roles can change you temporarily and forever at the same time. Small law firm attorneys are often underrepresented in leadership roles in the legal community (and all communities) because taking on more commitments is daunting. The pros and cons are equalized when you are operating from a clear vision of how leadership roles will add to your career. Using this viewpoint, it is easier to vet opportunities to determine if a short-term sacrifice is worth a long-term legacy.

Attorneys who are leaders have their own style that pairs up with the qualities they outwardly exhibit. A leadership style can be learned from others through having a great mentor or volunteering in a position that requires managing others. Some follow leadership-centered podcasts or seek out TED talks to develop in this area. Others seek out one-on-one coaching or devour leadership books. To become a leader in a community is a process of obtaining the skills and experience necessary to grow. The methods that you use to lead can be learned, and the characteristics of how you lead show an investment in yourself.

Varying your experiences outside your law firm through business development and community engagement will also help your leadership style develop. Some attorneys lead best by working directly with the community in a hands-on manner. For them, leadership can be exhibited through standing up for one family or a social cause or even through bridging communication with people with opposing views. The nonprofit sector is another area where lawyers can discover their leadership styles and qualities. Lawyers on the board of a philanthropic organization can start from a place of commitment to a mission or group of people. But through service with that nonprofit, they can reach higher to inspire changes to make the organization better and stronger, including the development of policies, ethics audits, and legal audits. Depending on their expertise, they might steer the nonprofit toward environmentally sustainable practices or changes in its fundraising procedures.

Regardless of the type of leader that you become, there are fundamental qualities that you should commit to so you can be more effective in your role.

Be Open-Minded

The legal industry has most of us looking at our time by the minute. You will need to spend what will feel like a lot of your professional time in your leadership roles, and this is not a waste. Being open-minded is as internal as it is external. Remind yourself that you are investing your time in yourself and your career through these commitments and experiences. This shift in mentality to be more open is imperative to keeping you engaged in work that will not have an "hours spent to dollars earned" profit margin. It will also ensure that you show up to events more receptive and hospitable, leading to meaningful connections.

Be Benevolent

Sound decisions are balanced by empathy and purpose. Developing your emotional intelligence is an imperative part of leadership that will guide you through a variety of interpersonal relationships in your professional world. Being a good leader is different from being a good lawyer. You didn't wake up with a JD, and you won't wake up a kind and thoughtful leader. It will take intention and effort to master benevolence as a leadership quality. Benevolence is shown by lawyers through consideration—being genuinely receptive to what others think. It is also shown through action—being consistent in how you spend your time, effort, and energy can show a track record of benevolence in a solo or small law firm.

Be Authentic

If you pursue an esteemed position in any community solely for the accolade, it will show. Leadership positions come with a laundry list of additional stresses and responsibilities. Those strains pile up, seemingly at the most inopportune time possible, leaving even the most committed lawyer feeling burned out. If the passion that brought you into the community or the cause to begin with is authentic, it helps protect against exhaustion. That original investment into the issues or the people that you intend to serve through your leadership position will support you through the highs and the lows of being a leader. Trying to take on an identity that isn't sincere will leave you irritated, bored, unengaged, and possibly resentful.

Persistent negative feelings will affect how you engage with others and how you lead, which can lead to a negative professional reputation.

PATHWAYS TO LEADERSHIP

A branded leadership path stays true to your core values and mission and helps you answer the question: how do you want your law practice to be of service to the community? The goal of leadership isn't necessarily running an organization or initiating a new project. Remember, leaders fill holes, and they look for opportunities to contribute. The path to leadership is not filled with empty activity to pursue the most esteemed title available but rather a true commitment to a community or a cause.

Leaders do take on added stress and responsibility in their professional lives, but usually, it is not all at once. Cultivating leadership is an aspect of your business development, and it is a process. Just as a plant has stages of growth, your leadership process will have different phases. Establishing yourself in your community, in your practice area, or in your niche takes time. What's nice is that along the way, you are growing as a professional and preparing yourself, along with your resume, for future engagements, dream clients, and leadership roles.

Nurturing your career through leadership involves taking responsibility for your reputation and your continued education. This will involve ongoing training and networking at a minimum. Getting better at anything takes effort and direction. For some, it might start small with a better handle on time management or communication skills. For others, improvement might be needed in trial skills, media training, or cultural sensitivity. You should be straightforward with yourself about where the deficiencies are in your resume or skill set. Leaders in any sector, including law, are shaped and developed. You might need to reverse engineer the goal of being a better community leader by updating your active listening skills, or finding ways that you can become better at introducing yourself to new connections. No one is born professionally evolved; leadership is a learnable skill.

Growth and professional improvement are linked to new experiences. Taking yourself out of your comfort zone through volunteer opportunities, short-term projects, and the like opens your eyes to different perspectives. These activities can also open your eyes to your hidden leadership talents. Sharpening your skills related to strategy, motivation, and communication contributes to how you will lead in your own organization as well as to your own networking and business development.

Your personal network can be activated in this area, too. Your network is a great place for feedback from other professionals in your network that you respect. This can be a formal plan with a mentor or a more casual brainstorming session with one of your colleagues over coffee. You can learn a ton from other people, helping you further your personal development and growth. Additionally, there is much to be learned from meeting with the existing leadership in a community. A good place to start would be bar association leadership or business community leaders. A quick email introduction takes under 15 minutes to research, write, send, and schedule a reminder for follow-up. Another idea would be to connect with religious leaders and community activists to talk to the top voices and learn from them, not get from them.

The road to becoming a leader is long. Professional leadership is a learned skill set. Attorneys at any stage of their careers can learn how to inspire others and follow a vision. But don't wait around for a leadership opportunity to fall in your lap; there will be small but defining moments over the course of your career where you can step up so you can stand out. Leadership takes a bit of risk to acquire, and one of its many rewards is humility. You will feel uncomfortable the first time you request donations for a nonprofit that you care deeply about; you might feel nervous the first time that you give a speech to a crowd of people who are also a crowd of potential client referral sources. But the more you do it, the better you get. It is true that you only must do it for the first time, one time. It gets easier with preparation and practice.

Take your own initiative to determine where you are stale or light in your skill set. Find the resources you have around you.

These can be revealed in opportunities for service to others or through self-education through common avenues such as books and lectures. Based on your time commitments and personal goals, you can then determine your unique strategy for leadership and growth.

CONSIDERATIONS IN LEADERSHIP ROLES

Chances are, when you become more immersed in a community, you will see the different ways that you can lead or contribute to positive change. It will be important to vet leadership opportunities through a lens specific to small law firm realities and challenges. When taking on a new leadership role, two vitally important considerations are boundaries and habits.

Boundaries

A repeating issue for attorneys involved in community activities and efforts is the lack of boundaries when it comes to leadership. Only you can answer the question of what meaningful engagement means to you and your law firm. You cannot be everything to everyone, and in leadership roles, there can be a lot of people putting items on your plate all at once. Being realistic about the time you must commit to a leadership opportunity will be a great way to keep you sane and on track while you execute your strategy.

Setting boundaries for your business development and adjusting them to include realistic blocks of time for leadership positions starts with a review of your calendar, time entries, and priorities for your law firm. Then, you can be realistic about the time you can devote to others. If you only have an extra few days or even a few hours every month, your service projects should respect and reflect that. If these are your time constraints, a bar association presidency might not be in your cards, but a few volunteer projects might be, or even management of a large financial project or gala spread out over months could be a better fit.

GOOD THINKING

Many professionals, including attorneys, find it efficient to plan their workdays in blocks, allowing them to clearly allocate time for community leadership work. "Time blocking is a time management technique that encourages you to schedule dedicated blocks of time for specific activities or tasks. It helps you focus on one task at a time, minimizing distractions and boosting productivity."[1]

For example, an attorney looking to time block to ensure they have space for leadership in their day could generally outline their daily schedule like the following:

8:00 am–9:00 am:	Review and Respond to Email and Emergencies
9:00 am–12:00 pm:	Billable Time/Case Work
12:00 pm–1:30 pm:	Break (lunch/workout/mindless scrolling)
1:30 pm–3:30 pm:	Billable Time/Case Work
3:30 pm–4:00 pm:	Review and Respond to Email and Emergencies
4:00 pm–6:30 pm:	Business Development/Community/Networking

Committing to a schedule like this one lets you carve out an extra ten-plus hours per week to work on your business development, which could include leadership obligations. This can be a challenge for courtroom lawyers who jump from hearings throughout the day, but it isn't impossible. Time blocking can look like saving chunks of hours to do business development on certain days—say Mondays and Fridays—and then handle hearings the rest of the week. When you control your day through time blocking, you insert boundaries

[1] https://www.mindjournals.com/blogs/read/what-is-time-blocking#:~:text=Time%20blocking%20is%20a%20time,Sounds%20good%20on%20paper.

regarding how much time you have for projects. Time management makes you more effective, and you will get more done.

Blocking your time allows you to control your day. It also helps you ensure that your goals and priorities related to the financial aspects of your day or billable time are accounted for, along with time to work out or even just do nothing—maybe you like to scroll through reels on YouTube to cleanse your mental palate midday. Others might enjoy watching reruns of 90s sitcoms on their phone during lunch to reset and decompress. Planning for time to be responsible for absolutely nothing matters—you will always find ways to be distracted and take a break regardless of whether you plan for it or not. Be smart and carve out this time intentionally in your schedule. Managing your time lets you hit your business development goals, which might include demanding leadership positions that require extended blocks of time to focus.

After a review of their time boundaries, some lawyers find that they only have a few days here and there during the month to be of service—or they devote a week or two to big service projects twice a year in their target communities or industries. This varied schedule works, too, as "helping hand" tasks and projects that are available for only a short amount can insert leadership into your career and CV quickly. For example, you might reflect on your community's surroundings and recognize that you can co-host a winter clothing drive with your bar association benefiting single-parent households. This leadership exercise doesn't take much time and will spread the word about your family law legal services while showcasing your commitment to the community.

Leadership means showing up for causes you believe in that are connected to your law firm's target audience or business development goals. Civil rights lawyers can inspire others to march with their firms in annual Dr. Martin Luther King Jr. events. This looks different from a business lawyer sharing insight and information with students at the local business school as a guest lecturer or providing pro bono representation to a struggling business. Being proactive with a service mindset is key. You don't have to spend a ton of money or time cultivating leadership in your life; you can start now where you are. *When it comes to leadership for your law practice, start small, start big, just start.*

But time isn't the only boundary to consider when it comes to leadership positions in your business development. Professional boundaries for any position, even those connected to the community and business development through the volunteer world, are just as important. Many attorneys go into leadership roles, such as serving a term as president of a bar association, with dreams of grand change, themes, and personal impact. Many are surprised to see that their tenure of leadership is over before they know it.

Even as the leader of an entire organization, it will be difficult to engage in lasting organizational or societal change if you only have a short amount of time. Organizational change is difficult to effectuate in a year, let alone in a year where you will be spread thin having a hand in an organization's operations that can include finances, dues, marketing, events, fundraising, and public relations.

GOOD THINKING

Remember that as a leader, you are not just in charge, but a steward of the organization you are leading, an ambassador. You aren't on the hook for its entire legacy. But you are on the hook for yours. Pay attention to your year or your term. That's all you can control, and it's a responsibility you should take seriously.

There will be pressure to address the organization's long-term goals or even past mistakes, but that cannot be accomplished in a one-year term. While you can maintain the vision and direction for the organization while you are at the helm, save your energy for shorter-term goals that you can act on in 6 to 12 months and determine your strategy for sharing updates and progress with the organization and its members. Having a realistic viewpoint of your volunteer term within the more extensive history of the organization will help you balance short-term and long-term goals.

Adding anything to the leadership commitments that you maintain outside your law practice, including initiatives unique to you or to your term as a leader, can be a lot to handle. To ensure that leadership roles and goals are feasible, set boundaries from the outset. Consider the following:

- When are you available to the organization?
- What are your expectations of others in the organization?
- What can you delegate or automate?
- How does the organization's mission align with your law practice's mission or your personal brand?
- At the end of your tenure or term, what do you want to be true about your impact?

Habits

Sitting at the top of any organization as a leader in any capacity will increase your professional visibility. This will directly affect your law firm's business development and, if you are playing your cards right, client acquisition. As a leader, you must develop healthy professional habits, including time management, and set professional boundaries, as previously discussed. But you will also want to pay attention to your marketing along the way and adopt habits that directly contribute to your leadership success.

Habit #1: Update Your Biography

The practice of law can be traced back to Ancient Rome and Greece. After all these years of attorneys practicing law, society has spoken: people choose lawyers; they don't choose law firms. The two most visited pages on any law firm's website are the home page and the attorney biography pages, the marketing data showing that "80% of legal website traffic goes to biographies."[2] This confirms from a data perspective what the legal industry has known for years—clients,

---

[2] https://www.consultwebs.com/blog/attorney-bio/#:~:text=As%20mentioned%20above%2C%2080%25%20of,on%20the%20Google%20results%20page.

even sophisticated ones, want to have a connection with the person or team that is handling their legal issues. If you know in advance that there will be more people looking at your website or when embarking on a business development strategy that will increase your personal visibility, be sure to keep your law firm website biography updated.

Professional services like legal services are a relationship game. An updated attorney biography on a website can bridge a connection between you and your target audience and the legal services you provide. It can help answer their questions about why you are the best advocate in their situation. An outdated biography, on the other hand, can give a message of staleness. Maintaining your biography doesn't have to be hard and is an easy project to delegate to someone non-billable in your office or even a vendor you hire hourly to handle it.

Biographies that are drafted with the audience in mind are not big blocks of hard-to-read text. White space is used throughout a well-drafted biography to encourage readability, along with the use of clear categories for organizing the information. These categories have different naming conventions depending on the practice of the attorney. However, a "professional activity" area is usually associated with bar association membership, leadership in industry activities, and so on. A "community affiliations" area can be used to display nonprofit work concerning social causes, including community board activities. Many law firms without a dedicated marketing professional will overlook adding membership of specific committees within a bigger organization and timeframes of service. This is a mistake, as you will have every intention of remembering what you are up to, but it is easy to forget what year you became the "chair of so and so" after the time has passed. It is smart to update that information in real time or keep a repository of notes to update your biography quarterly. A reminder on your calendar once per quarter is a helpful nudge to keep this area updated. If you consistently pay attention to your biography, it will never be outdated. Your marketing will always be ready to support your business development success in leadership roles.

Habit #2: Plan Ahead for Follow-Up

Having a leadership role can make many things possible for a solo or small law practice. While you are in the moment, it will feel like there are an endless number of meet-and-greets, galas, happy hours, and other meetings to attend. The time will feel busy and rushed, and it will go fast. But this chaos has a time limit and a shelf-life. The intense visibility and activity associated with leading an organization outside your own business can and will end, so take advantage of it and prepare before you begin.

Have a plan for how you will keep in contact with the new connections you are interacting with. Some attorneys automatically send everyone to their LinkedIn profile to stay connected. Through that platform, their network sees weekly information on their law practice and how the leadership roles or community work talk to their day job as a lawyer in a B2B or B2C practice area. Through LinkedIn, they not only stay at the top of the minds of the people they meet throughout the year, but they also continually remind them through positive association of how they help and serve. LinkedIn is one of many follow-up options. Other attorneys might use a CRM system for relationship building. Another effective strategy is an email newsletter, which ensures ongoing visibility and engagement with your network.

Habit #3: Share Your Success

Solo practices and small law firms must toot their own horns. If you don't share what is going on in your law firm, no one will know. Regularly promoting your successes and celebrating your wins is a key aspect of getting more for your small law firm from leadership roles. Taking on leadership roles equips you with credentials that other lawyers might not have. A built-out CV takes the intention to collect information piece-by-piece. This happens through micro-updates like the ones suggested earlier, with once-per-quarter biography updates. Savvy attorneys make a regular plan to keep track of what they are doing, including lectures, awards, publications, case wins, community service, and interviews with the press. They also have a coordinated plan to follow up.

A key part of promoting your work, leadership, and other career successes is having a personal promotional strategy. Even if it is a small plan or just a few bullet points to keep you consistent, you need a way to announce the great things you have been up to in your career. Attorneys can add information about their community service projects and leadership positions to their existing marketing campaigns. This isn't bragging; rather, it is great fodder for a small law firm to compete with larger firms that absolutely engage in this type of promotion. LinkedIn is the perfect place for a few poignant posts to confirm the bridge between your community leadership and the impact it makes on your target audience or legal issue. Another idea is steadily adding blog posts to your website regarding your leadership roles. Consistent blogging is a habit that supports the health of your law firm's website. Consider that "Google generally crawls a website anywhere from once every three days to four weeks."[3] By providing the hungry algorithm with something on-topic to read about your firm, you meet its content needs and are rewarded with elevated rankings and visibility on your website. Again, blog posts are helpful from a digital marketing and business development perspective. They can be repurposed on social media for your network of clients and referral sources. Chances are some of these ideas will work to add to your promotional plan.

REAL-WORLD ETHICS

Consider a scenario where a solo practice attorney is running a campaign to be elected as a school board member in their community. This attorney is passionate about protecting student rights in the public school system. They are interested in board membership as it aligns perfectly with their brand and law firm goals, especially regarding audience, impact, credentialing, and visibility. As they run their campaign on a small budget, there is zero money to spend on an external public relations team or ethics counsel for oversight.

---

[3] https://linkwhisper.com/how-often-does-google-crawl-a-site/#:~:text=These%20are%20two%20important%20questions,factors%20which%20I%20will%20discuss.

To offset costs, the attorney consumed hours of free public relations video content published on social media platforms by internet "experts" on campaign strategy. These videos share broad tips on how to run a school board campaign and win. The lawyer in this situation is a practicing lawyer *and* a candidate for a school board position. *It's crucial that they review information regarding marketing, solicitation, and communication in the states where they are admitted to proceed with caution and ensure compliance.*

***

Solo and small firm attorneys have dual roles when they take on leadership positions in the community. They are not only leading the operations in their own shop but also branching out to impact the greater community, inside and outside the legal industry. There are many pathways to leadership for practicing lawyers, and some start with a decision to create a long-term legacy for their practice. For others, the decision feels made for them, and leadership opportunities evolve more organically for their practice. Regardless of how you get there, leadership can take your small law firm to the next level. Leadership roles can bring immense visibility to your career with long-term benefits, including ongoing respect and prestige—especially for bar association presidents.

Leadership roles will change you and make you a better professional. As a steward of any organization, you will grow into the position, which will augment your perspective on many levels. The examples of personal growth for lawyers who lead are endless, as they all stem from activities that are unique to the individual. However, what is the same for everyone is the need for clear boundaries and productive habits to insulate your leadership roles from engagement erosion or, even worse, feeling used.

Lawyers who lead can be amazing at showing up for others and bad at showing up for themselves. They are some of the worst offenders when it comes to telling the world about the good things they do in the community. For some, this type of promotion feels like bragging, which might be the exact opposite of why they are involved in leadership efforts to begin with. Consider there are many ways to show humility in your law practice and professional life. However, having an outdated biography is not one of them. Keeping your own records, including your website biography, updated and finding ways to share how you mix your passion with your profession will earn you more visibility from leadership commitments.

With a clear strategy on what impact you want to see on the community and your career, leadership roles are a smart move for solo and small law firms. Executed correctly, they can work in conjunction with a B2B and or B2C law practice to provide great visibility and promotion.

5

Commitment

> *Commitment is an act, not a word.*
>
> **—Jean-Paul Sartre**

Commitment is the cornerstone of a successful business development strategy. Much planning and dedication are necessary to execute a business development plan effectively. Small law firm lawyers, who often juggle multiple roles, will find valuable insights on how to carve out time for business development every week and consistently track progress. Solo and small firm attorneys can struggle with time management issues, particularly when it comes to non-billable tasks like business development and marketing. This chapter delves into the need for balanced time commitments and consistency in business development. By implementing actionable and productive time management strategies, you can regain control and empower yourself to meet your business development goals.

***

Even when they work for someone else, successful attorneys take responsibility for their own law practices and have plans for their business development. This entrepreneurial mindset is key to keeping them hungry and engaged throughout their careers. Most attorney business development plans start with the foundational items we have discussed in this book—finding a niche, developing a mission, and determining which professional circles and leadership roles will best support their goals. They then curate these items into one executable strategy that they follow diligently every week and month.

What is missing from the simplicity of these steps is the commitment it takes to stay focused and engaged with a business development strategy. As a solo practitioner or small law firm attorney, you are responsible for many things. On any given day, there are tiny crises to handle in your business and for your clients in your law practice. These situations can feel unpredictable as they eat your time while they eat your peace. So, you have great intentions, and you set big goals. You make big transformative promises to yourself about your law practice and its legacy, and then you break them.

We have all done it before, starting a new shiny project with the best intentions of making your professional life better or more focused in the direction you have always wanted. You set goals, you start routines, and you feel like a million bucks—for a few weeks. And then the reality sets in, the real you takes over—the one who doesn't want to set up coffee commitments to connect with new contacts or write a blog post after a long day of work. The plan that you worked so hard to develop falls flat because you are your own everything in a small law firm. You are your marketing team, your business coach, your HR, and your accounting team all at once. There are only so many hours in a day, and determining how you will use these hours wisely and incorporate them into your business development—even when you are exhausted or drained—is vital when putting together your strategy and your plan to execute. Business development strategies look great on paper, but without the action plan backed up by tactical daily and weekly tasks needed to support them, they are just a pipedream.

COMMITTED TO COMMITMENTS

The magic in connecting the dots between your hopes and dreams and the reality of your legal career is found in the commitment.

Professional success and development are earned. The same mentality of hitting the gym consistently to see results works here. Ask any successful attorney what they have sacrificed to get where they are, and you will consistently hear of personal sacrifices they have made through long nights and missed fun. Just as you can't expect six-pack abs after one workout session, you can't show up to one professional event every three months, talk to no one, and expect results. However, understanding how to commit can increase your chances of succeeding in attaining your professional goals. Realistic goals address personal downfalls that stomp out any fire that business development starts. A plan within your business development strategy for combating laziness, boredom, and other forms of resistance that are common in the legal industry is a must-have.

Set Financial Limits

We naturally consider the financial part of business development as the bottom line or the most important component or consideration in planning. In a small law firm setting, your bottom line when it comes to business development isn't just about money. Your plan must acknowledge personal considerations, such as your time and energy, through a realistic lens. Consider that much of the way we communicate is nonverbal; about 55 percent of communication is nonverbal.[1] If you are a litigator, is it realistic to plan to attend a happy hour and show up with the energy needed to connect with new colleagues after a full day of taking depositions? Or, if you are an introvert, is it realistic to have in your business development plan that you will attend weekly in-person networking events?

Lawyers who start with a realistic plan reach their goals. Business development strategies that aren't well thought out and are rushed, poorly designed, or ignored when it comes to execution fail—plain and simple. Ensure that your strategy and goals are both

---

[1] https://online.utpb.edu/about-us/articles/communication/how-much-of-communication-is-nonverbal/#:~:text=The%2055%2F38%2F7%20Formula&text=It%20was%20Albert%20Mehrabian%2C%20a,%2C%20and%207%25%20words%20only.

realistic and based on an achievable execution plan. Creating a high-reaching strategy is easier when you divide monster business development goals into smaller milestones to be achieved. For example, if you would like to be a bar association president one day, this is a realistic goal if you are willing to take the necessary smaller steps to achieve it.

Look at your business development and personal marketing budget for the year before deciding how much activity they can realistically support in a year. You must consider what percentage of your income, or the firm's income, will be earmarked for business development. It is true that an ABA survey in 2020 found that "less than half of law firms of all sizes have a marketing budget."[2] So you might be starting from scratch, and if you are, be sure to include common items that will come up during business development and personal marketing. These include money for sponsorship, graphic design for advertisement, and contribution of swag items, along with smaller costs that come with meeting folks for coffee or picking up lunch when you invite a prospect out. All this adds up, and a budget is an important part of making sure you are mindful of the costs associated with backing up your plan and your goals and a smarter way to start.

Reduce Resistance

Being realistic about how you will commit to your business development strategy includes a plan for hard days, bad moments, and even failure. The confidence you build when planning and strategizing doesn't necessarily show up for you every day. There will be days and sometimes months when you question yourself and your business development strategy. Achieving business success as a lawyer is not a linear process. This resistance is part of growth.

Healthy habits to address resistance in attorney business development look like new systems:

---

[2] https://www.americanbar.org/groups/law_practice/resources/tech-report/archive/websites-marketing/.

- To-do lists.
  - Make to-do lists every day and every week with the most urgent tasks listed first.
  - Consistently review time constraints and deadlines.
- Communication channels.
  - Review email only twice per day.
  - Review LinkedIn twice per week.
- Delegation and automation.
  - Scheduling and calendaring.
  - Community outreach.
  - Social media posting.

Your professional world feels less chaotic when you have consistency and routine through daily, weekly, and monthly habits. To flesh out these habits, a bit of preparation can be helpful. It can work to look at your plan through a lens of, "How can I make any of this easier on myself?" Just as studies show that creating personal systems helps keep you on track for healthy eating and exercise, the same is true when it comes to navigating roadblocks in business development. If you have the full event schedule printed and ready for review, it is more probable that you will attend a conference with great business development potential. *Print it.*

The same goes for time blocking. Some of the biggest names in the world, including Elon Musk, use time-blocking techniques.[3] This productivity method shields your productivity by controlling your calendar and creating dedicated blocks of focus in your week. Being intentional with your time will prevent the damage caused to your business development strategy by weekly "winging it" when it comes to your goals. *Calendar it.*

Distractions and resistance don't belong in your professional world. By looking at your plan through the lens of how to make it easy on yourself, you can resist the temptation to abandon goals for that day, that week, or even altogether. Breaking larger goals down

[3] https://yourstory.com/2023/11/elon-musk-5-minute-rule-increases-productivity.

into smaller tasks helps, but when those tasks are repeatable, they become patterns. Habits in attorney business development boost productivity and lower stress. They likewise reduce resistance.

Energy for Activity

At some point in your planning process, you must ask yourself, what are you good at? Or even, what business development activities do you enjoy the most? The honest answers to these basic questions lay out activities that give you energy and those that drain it into two easy categories. Professional networking and business development don't necessarily occur during normal business hours. They don't necessarily occur when you have a clear schedule with lots of time to meet new connections or the energy required for leadership work. Committing to your law firm's business development goals is made easier when you add your fundamental interests, talents, and abilities into the mix. Attaining your goals in business development should not feel forced. There are plenty of ways to intentionally insert activities into the strategy that you enjoy. You are likelier to continue networking activities that are easy for you to handle rather than those that you dread doing.

Consider these common areas of internal pushback and the suggested workarounds:

- **Dislike networking alone?** Develop a short list of colleagues you can invite to events with you. Ensure you have a business development mindset when you are brainstorming which colleagues are the right fit. Do they help and serve a similar audience as you? Who do they know within the industry or group they can introduce you to at the event? Is there any synergy between what you both do for a living that would interest the event attendees?
- **Dislike writing projects?** Lawyers can be thought leaders in many ways, including through publishing articles and white papers. But some attorneys write so much daily that they can't stand the idea of taking on additional writing projects

> for business development. For these lawyers, their business development strategies might include credentialing and visibility in different formats than publishing. They might enjoy giving lunch and learns that run on a predictable format, so they create visibility through an hour of public speaking. They might take on a committee role in a professional organization rather than signing up to do blog posting in their newsletters.

We all have strengths and weaknesses in our personalities that can affect our professional successes if we let them. Skills that need more development can be addressed through education and training. A fear of public speaking can be overcome through consistency and practice—or public speaking can be mostly avoided in a business development strategy mindful of your strengths and preferences. What is brilliant about small law firm business development is that it is tailored to you. Knowing what you are good at and building a business development strategy with tactical activities removes the resistance from your business development. Repeating business development activities that you enjoy levels up your confidence, which will increase your openness to take on new challenges and risks, leading to better opportunities for your law practice. It also ensures that you bring more positive energy to your tasks, lessening the feelings of reluctance that can stop a business development strategy before it even begins.

***

Solo and small law firm attorneys must plan for their success regarding the commitment required to develop and execute a business development plan. You must keep yourself on track. Tactical activities keep the daily and weekly activities moving and lead to achieving bigger career goals. The reality is that you can have the best intentions with the greatest plan in the world drafted, but if you don't commit at all levels—financial and otherwise—the efforts fall flat. Reviewing your habits and systems related to business development through a critical eye ensures you stay focused and on the right path.

6

Create

> *We are what we repeatedly do.*
>
> **—Aristotle**

Long-term goals can be broken down into short-term goal setting, allowing for new habits to form a consistent routine in business development. This chapter works with attorneys who have read through the previous foundational chapters or are ready to create a new business development strategy. This discussion also applies to lawyers who have a great business development plan but are struggling to execute it.

***

There is no one to farm your business development plan out to when you are in a solo practice or a small law firm. Regardless of your end goal in business development, it will be hard work to make it happen. When you own your own firm or work in a small firm, there is no one to blame if the business development goals aren't met. If you want your business development to skyrocket, you need to set realistic goals and work on them consistently. You must stick to your plan and not be distracted, as there will be hurdles, and the commitment killers are endless. There is nothing certain here to rely on but your own actions for attaining your goals and securing your results.

YOUR BUSINESS DEVELOPMENT STRATEGY V. YOUR TACTICAL PLAN

Your strategy is your blueprint. If you are taking the time to plot out what type of career success you want or what type of professional legacy you want to leave, ensure that your strategy stays top of mind in your daily, weekly, and monthly decisions through a tactical plan. This tactical plan lays out the actual activities that support your blueprint or strategy.

GOOD THINKING

Your strategy lays out your law firm or practice's goals and objectives; your tactical plan is how you will bring them to life. This planning is key to your business development success as it will help you think through your goals, anticipate challenges, and develop benchmarks for success. Leading researchers have confirmed that successful goal-setting rests on the motivation and consistency that planning provides. A 2019 PwC survey found that "companies that invest more time and effort into strategy execution are three times more likely to report above-average growth and twice as likely to report above-average profits than those that don't."[1] In a nutshell, this won't happen on its own. It is important to take the time to plan out your success.

With a business development plan, you have the roadmap needed for true professional growth and business development success. With a corresponding tactical plan, there is nowhere to hide; when you are

---

[1] https://www.strategyand.pwc.com/gx/en/unique-solutions/cds/the-strategy-crisis.pdf.

looking at a predetermined task list, you know what you took care of that week and what you didn't. Your business development plan will include many moving pieces. The financial part of execution, in addition to the tactical activities required, can be a blind spot for small businesses. To stay engaged with the plan that you create to back up your law firm business development strategy, think it through.

Your Business Development Strategy

Your strategy is at the foundation of your solo or small law firm's business development. Just as there is one business plan for your firm, there is one business development plan for your firm or for your individual practice within a small law firm. This business development strategy is alive; it is adaptable. This fluidity is important, as you don't know what you don't know, and there is a bit of mystery in everyone's career. There will be moments that you didn't see coming and people that you never dreamed you would have the chance to be around. You might begin your career as a corporate law attorney doing outside general counsel work. But you might settle into a profitable niche working with healthcare entrepreneurs or with local hospitality groups or even meet your goal of running your own legal department one day as general counsel.

Your business development strategy ensures that your professional behaviors match up with your personal beliefs and goals. It serves as bumper rails and a compass for your law practice at the same time. Your strategy provides a structure to address the areas of achievement that are important to you. Yet, it is necessarily organic to accommodate new opportunities that come from sustained energy and visibility.

GOOD THINKING

Review your business development strategy at least once yearly, and in an ideal world, two times a year. You need to keep your purpose, brand, and goals top of mind; the only way to do that is to remind yourself.

(Continued)

> ***Put your oxygen mask on and update your calendar or your tickle system with your business development tasks from your tactical plan so you stay accountable and on track. Attorneys can easily use reminder systems in Microsoft and Outlook as well as task management systems such as ClickUp or Todoist to stay the course.***

Your underlying strategy reflects your brand, goals, and passions. Because it is unique to you, it helps with short-term and long-term decision-making because it is always there to compare any opportunity against.

- Does joining this organization make sense *with your strategy*?
- Does sponsoring this event place you in front of the target audience *in your strategy*?
- Does taking on this short-term leadership role conform with *your long-term strategy*?

Having a business development strategy makes planning easier for your law firm. When you rely on a business development strategy for your small law firm, your target is steady, and you are invested in the patterns and activities that will support attaining specific goals through activities centered around energy and initiative, as well as consistent frequency. It is easier to discern what activities are best for your law firm rather than trying to make a case-by-case decision focused on a moving target.

Your Tactical Plan

Smart business development plans for small law firms should lay out the processes and procedures needed to execute the same. For example, if your firm has a goal of connecting with your new business development contacts using LinkedIn, you should also have it in your plan to be on LinkedIn consistently. Deciding to send a connection request without any idea of why you are using LinkedIn as part of your business development wastes your time and theirs. Rather, if you are taking the time to seek out new people in your network on LinkedIn to stay connected and visible in their worlds, ensure that your tactical plan is how you will keep your profile updated and what type of posting cadence your audience will see.

Financial Considerations

It can be exciting to learn how to differentiate a business development strategy (the blueprint) from a tactical plan (the trackable tasks needed to follow the blueprint) for your law firm. But remember, strategy comes first in the process and is then followed by the tactical plan to execute the goals, and there will be financial considerations that have to be determined in advance and can only be determined by you.

Your business development plan must be rooted in the reality of your law firm's finances. In law, time is literally money, so having a handle on what type of time and financial commitments you need to make related to business development will help keep you on the right path. For example, if you block out two hours every single Tuesday and Thursday afternoon to commit a total of four hours a week to bar association activities or developing new legal services for your niche, it is more helpful to know in advance if that is time you will have to make up on other days of the week or if it is a foreseeable loss that you can build into your law firm's finances.

WHAT SHOULD A BUSINESS DEVELOPMENT STRATEGY AND TACTICAL PLAN LOOK LIKE?

Strategy and plan should not feel like imposing terms. There is no right or wrong way to format your business development strategy, plan, tasks, and associated ideas. Everyone's business development strategy and plan will look different. For some, it is a document on their computer that they refer to once a quarter to ensure they stay on track. For others, it is calendared tasks that back up their bigger goals that they load into their daily workload. There are plenty of software options out there to help solo practitioners and small law firm attorneys with the reminders needed to stay on schedule.

B2B SPOTLIGHT: BUSINESS DEVELOPMENT STRATEGY FOR LITIGATOR ADDING ADR TO PRACTICE

A litigator has created a credentialed career in the courtroom with the intention of adding an alternative dispute resolution (ADR) component to their practice. This litigator must be credentialed in ADR before they can begin taking those matters on. This attorney also intends to create more visibility in their law practice with other litigators as a funnel for the eventual ADR work.

They could break down this business development strategy with the initial tasks (outlined next) to be tracked for completion in 12 months broken down by fiscal quarter:

Business Development Strategy

Strategy:	Transition litigation practice to include ADR services
Audience:	Litigators
Tasks:	ADR certification

- Complete state bar association mediation and arbitration certification course. (Q1)

ADR experience

- Serve as a volunteer mediator with the local court focused on business disputes and civil conflicts. (Q2)
- Create and maintain a repository of ADR experience to eventually add to the firm's website, attorney biography, and other promotional materials to sell ADR services. (Q2-Q4)

ADR networking

- Schedule rotating coffees and lunches with local trial attorneys already in network to begin discussing the law firm's additional focus, ADR services.
- Begin to add and segment contacts in an email campaign for future ADR messaging.

In this example, the litigator makes headway on their goal of adding an ADR component to an existing litigation practice through deliberate trackable activities spread out over a year. They know that a new credential is required, so they sign up for that training. The attorney understands that they will need to build validation of their ADR services, so they are keeping an internal list of the ADR matters that they are handling. Finally, they begin chatting about their new practice area in their network while building a new email list to capture the audience.

GOOD THINKING

Email campaigns are an automatable way of staying in touch with your audience. It was found that "64% of small businesses use email marketing to reach customers." Email marketing will work for most, if not all, law firms, with even 81 percent of B2B marketers reporting that email newsletters are the best option to stay connected with their client base. [2]

Your law firm's email campaign can start small with current and past clients included and expand slowly by adding new clients as they open matters throughout the year.

When it comes to business developing strategy and planning, you can get bogged down in the look and feel of your plan. But don't let yourself get distracted by the presentation. That's not what matters. The key is having real-time accountability and execution when it comes to your business development plan. The format doesn't matter here—the commitment does.

WHERE TO START

Your business development strategy and tactical action plan blend the items you have previously decided to pursue for your practice. Committing to your success starts with having a clear vision of the

[2] https://blog.hubspot.com/marketing/email-marketing-stats#:~:text=Segmented%20emails%20drive%2030%25%20more,over%20the%20last%2012%20months.

end goal. If you want to be the top DUI attorney in your community, your entire strategy, including the weekly activities you plan to perform, should be focused on that end goal. Some attorneys might need more training in a certain area to keep their skills sharp or update their knowledge base, and that is a tangible task that, again, supports their end goals. For others, they might need to expand their networks to have more involvement with decision-makers and leaders related to their practice areas.

In a B2B scenario, a real estate lawyer wants to handle the transactional side of commercial transactions. If their network has gone stale, part of their strategy might include a deliberate process for meeting new people. To execute this task, they will attend industry events, connect with others on LinkedIn, ask for introductions in the community, and so on. The tasks that you need to handle to achieve a professional goal need to be laid out clearly: what steps do you need to take to achieve the end goal or even get a little closer to it over the next year?

Step 1: Prepare for Your Success

When you list the steps to be followed to achieve your goal, be specific: call this person and schedule lunch to take place this month, and contact "so and so" to request a lecture later in the year. Be sure to take note of any deadlines that might need to be considered and of any information that might need to be prepared beforehand. A good example would be a lawyer wanting to pitch themselves to be onstage at an upcoming conference but has not determined what the title of their lecture would be and why it pertains to the conference attendees. In another scenario, this might look like the lawyer wanting to lecture and successfully pitching the lecture but then feeling a scramble when it is time to provide a speaker biography or pay a graphic designer to create presentation slides. Because small law firms don't have huge business development and marketing teams, it is important that they get their ducks in a row before they need to be.

To achieve your goal, you will need resources handy, like an editable version of your CV or a canned list of presentations. Prepare for your success by creating specific tasks to be completed to support your business development goals.

Step 2: Consider Your Commitments

We have all been there, signing up six months in advance for an event that we dread attending and are considering ditching. Six months ago, it seemed fun and something you looked forward to attending. But the thought of leaving your office after an eight-hour day to attend a two-hour after-hours party now sounds like torture. Good intentions aren't enough in business development. There are countless excuses out there, especially in the small law firm world. Understanding your hurdles and roadblocks can help you devise a solid plan that will keep you motivated.

Common challenges include feeling overcommitted or even half-committed, but your plan can include ideas on how to keep your business development moving in the right direction. Feeling overcommitted comes when you have overpromised access to resources like your time. Overcommitment feels like drowning. Planning in advance how much time you can commit during your week to your business development puts more control over your calendar. Adding large time blocks ahead of time to ensure you have time for deep focus along with time to deal with emergencies will add sanity and structure to a busy calendar. To combat being overcommitted, some attorneys add a weekly review of their schedule and deliverables. Every Sunday evening, for example, they block out an hour to determine what is coming up for the next week so they can hit the ground running on Monday morning with an actionable list of tasks that need to be completed around their meetings.

Having too much on your plate through overcommitment feels like you are sinking, and the lack of fully committing to your strategy and your plan shows up as guilt. Having a business development plan for your law practice requires that you be tough on yourself to keep going. In an age of self-compassion, which allows us more wiggle room than ever, accountability in your professional life provides balance. You can be emotionally acceptable and flexible with yourself as you reach for your professional goals. But simultaneously, you must have systems and processes in place to ensure this accountability. To prevent a lapse in business development activity, a solo practice attorney might set aside money each month to save for a short vacation to reward themselves after all the hard work. Another idea would be to work toward a "me day," as after you expend a ton of time and energy in service to others, having a day to yourself during the week can feel like an oasis.

Deciding to develop an intentional business development strategy and to support that strategy through a niche, a brand, and your marketing takes work. But feeling half-committed to your goals or completing the tasks required to reach them is something only you can fix. Combat inevitable business development fatigue by preempting the unengaged moments. Remind yourself constantly of your mission and why that matters, keep score consistently of where you are at in your business development strategy so you can see progress, and don't forget to brainstorm a few positive ways of rewarding your effort.

Step 3: Accountability

Accountability in business development keeps you consistent. Attorneys have many options for accountability partners. In this regard, look for someone who is shooting for similar goals or even a mentor who has walked the path in their own career. Accountability partners need to meet with you consistently. They should be aware of what your bigger goals are and how you break them down into smaller tactical tasks. They won't know if you skip out on a networking event or if you have fallen behind on your blogging strategy, so you will need to insert honesty as an additional safeguard of your success. Even if you are cramming to meet the business development deadlines that you have set for yourself, being honest with your accountability partner about challenges can help. They are there to move your business development and support you through your tough moments, but their hands are tied if they don't have a truthful picture of what is going on.

Even with options available, most solo and small law firm attorneys pursue their business development goals independently, and everything about their business development will be up to them. An ABA report on the legal industry found, "Most solos (66%) do their own marketing, and over 73% of attorneys from firms of 2–8 and 10–49 lawyers say lawyers perform marketing tasks."[3] You might be your own accountability partner. And that's not a bad thing. You can create a business development strategy with a tactical plan that holds you accountable for achieving your goals. You might not have someone blowing a whistle at you every time you slow down, but you can watch your own numbers and celebrate your own wins. You can be your own cheerleader.

The easiest way to keep yourself on track is to develop KPIs or key performance indicators for your law practice. KPIs aren't just for big corporations or even big law firms; they work for everyone regardless of the size of your practice. KPIs measure your performance and keep your successes trackable. The land of business development and marketing can feel like a black hole that swallows the time and energy around it. With KPIs, you have quantifiable metrics that let you know how good, or not bad, you are doing in your law firm's relationships and business development projects.

KPIs create a defined path toward meeting your desired professional results. Without accountability in your strategy, you are less likely to predict that your activities will result in the outcomes you originally intended. For those looking for measurable metrics in their business development, a set of KPIs provides the answer.

KPIs are only as good as you let them be. They will provide you with clarity when it comes to measuring your project against your strategic objectives. They will also help you share your progress with others if you have a mentor or accountability group. This is especially helpful if you are in a small law firm, and you have someone above

---

[3] https://www.americanbar.org/groups/law_practice/resources/legal-technology-resource-center/tech-survey/2020/.

you or a business partner to report to. KPIs are great if you are a solo practitioner because they will alert you when action is needed in an area or when there is cause for celebration because you have hit a goal.

Developing your metrics for success through KPIs starts small. For example, a small law firm owner who works in the trusts and estates area sees the Clio Legal Trends Report's findings related to responding to client inquiries. This report found that "most clients (82%) agreed that timeliness was important [in response to the potential client's initial inquiry], and 79% indicated that they expected a response within 24 hours."[4] This attorney's personal brand includes aspects of respect for families, and devotion to their community members, so they are inspired to improve their response time for potential client inquiries through a simple KPI.

To do so, this firm would need to track the sales process from the first time the lead contacts the law firm to the time the law firm's attorney or staff returns the contact. Review the following example to see how a KPI is used to support a business development goal backed up by metrics. Their KPI would be the time between messages sent to the law firm minus the time the law firm took to respond. That equals their response time, which is a trackable metric that will determine how well or not the attorney is performing in this area.

Software and technology will be a big help in tracking your KPIs in addition to automation and delegation. This aspect of reporting is not necessarily high on the priority list for small and solo law firms, with an ABA report finding, "Only 17% of respondents reported that their firm received regular reports of marketing performance from their external agencies. Another 39% said they did not use an external agency. Twenty-one percent of respondents said their firms received regular reports of marketing performance from their internal marketing teams, and 42% said they did not have an internal

[4] https://www.clio.com/about/press/clios-legal-trends-report-reveals-law-firms-struggle-to-respond-to-client-inquiries/.

marketing team."[5] You will want to choose your platforms as carefully as you choose your staffing in this regard. For example, if you are going to track your own metrics on a spreadsheet, clearly define the roles, even yours, in when the numbers will be pulled and how, as well as who will update your spreadsheet. For KPIs to work, your success must be trackable, so make your process for gathering your data as clear as possible. The systems need to be easy to use to accommodate busy, unengaged, or even tired times that are inevitable.

When it comes to KPIs for your law firm, data can be pulled from several sources in addition to spreadsheets, and those sources will depend on what data you are trying to track. Common sources of pulling data related to your business development can come from tracking inquiries to your website and entries into a Customer Relationship Management system, or CRM.

B2C SPOTLIGHT: BUSINESS DEVELOPMENT FOR DUI DEFENSE PRACTICE

In this B2C example, a DUI defense attorney has a coordinated plan to reach their target audience and professional goals. The marketing tasks associated with business development are easily delegated or automated to ensure that the lawyer controls their time while staying connected to current and new contacts.

Additionally, this attorney engages in a reputation management campaign that helps its Google Business page stay healthy with updated feedback on their legal services from real clients. Additionally, the lawyer is visible to other attorneys and the community through in-person activities

(Continued)

[5] https://www.americanbar.org/groups/law_practice/resources/tech-report/2022/websites-marketing/.

> such as networking, board service, and lectures. These activities are chosen with the mindset of staying top of mind to referral sources for casework but also to attain third-party awards in the strategy that is based on peer voting.
>
> This simple B2C plan is repeatable and sustainable as it respects the lawyers' time boundaries and does not drain finances through expensive sponsorships or advertising. Rather, the marketing is laser-focused on supporting the in-person business development strategy, allowing for more delegation and automation of follow-up.

Business Development Strategy

Unique Value Proposition:	We protect the fair and equitable treatment of people who have been accused of breaking the law through intoxicated driving by providing excellent and empathetic legal defense.
Personal Brand:	Award-winning DUI defense attorney with great results who focuses on discreetly handling all aspects of DUI cases, including court and DMV hearings.
Practice Area Focus:	Criminal defense
Niche:	DUI defense
Target Audience:	Individuals 21–24 years old and their families in metro area surrounding the law firm for representation.[6] Bondspeople in and around the metro area for referrals. Criminal defense lawyers and business attorneys, as both do not practice DUI defense, for referrals.

[6] https://www.nhtsa.gov/risky-driving/drunk-driving#:~:text=In%202022%2C%20the%20highest%20percentage,for%20every%20female%20drunk%20driver.

Professional Goals: Profitable solo DUI law practice validated by case results, third-party awards, and client feedback.

Visibility in bar association related to criminal defense and DUI defense.

Tactical Activities

Professional Activity: Local criminal defense bar membership

State bar association membership

Board membership in local nonprofit

Community Efforts: Lunch-and-learn events

Networking

Time Block: Five hours per week on business development with two weeks off for vacation, sick time, and other incidentals

In-Person Activities: Attend state criminal defense bar association meetings and networking events in addition to serving on the leadership board of the DUI section to ensure visibility with criminal defense attorneys for case referrals.

Present regularly to business attorneys through the state bar on the leading ways that DUI charges can affect businesses and businesspeople.

Service on the board of a local nonprofit related to safe driving with a branded commitment to become a leader in the organization.

Rotating coffees and lunches with professional contacts and referral sources including those in the bail bonding industry.

Marketing Activities:	Three times per week, LinkedIn posts on issues related to DUI defense. Monthly email campaign to segmented lists providing proactive and positive information on various topics, including those related to safe driving and prevention of DUIs. Maintenance of a Google Business page for the law firm to collect client and colleague feedback whenever possible on the law firm's customer service and results.

DON'T LOOK FOR A SHORTCUT

When it comes to enjoying the relationships that come from business development, there isn't an easy button. You must earn these relationships over time through consistent, sincere, and branded activities. Remember, you aren't the only attorney trying to meet these people, do business with them, and so on. You cannot shortcut this success. If you aren't seeing the results you want or the results that you predicted would be true by a certain time, make sure that you pause to reevaluate your actions and your plan. What is working? What isn't? Do you need to refresh your plan or add some new people to your network? Long-term business development takes time. For people who are geared toward impatience, this can be a frustrating road to be on. If you go to an event or even five events, and you don't have any new movement in your business development, take a minute to reflect on your behavior and the event itself: was your target audience in attendance; were you open to meeting new people and following your plan for connecting? Usually, through realistic reflection of our own behaviors, in addition to double-checking the audience we are in front of, we can see what might need to be changed or tweaked along the way.

Business development is a process for everyone—even the people who make it look easy and effortless. But it can be learned. Be kind to yourself as you are navigating the business development "ropes" for your practice. You are literally writing your own playbook as you go, and that takes effort along with trial and error. Learn from your failures and keep your mindset driven and focused as you adopt a proactive attitude that doesn't allow excuses. If you commit to four hours a week of personal marketing and business development, do it. There are plenty of other lawyers out there who are making the sacrifices now to enjoy bigger books of business later.

Dodge these disruptions by surrounding yourself with people who are on your level—people who are changing their lives, people who are growing, and people who have the same positive momentum that you do. If you have colleagues who get together to gripe about what is bad through venting or gossip about others in the legal community, skip those meetings. These types of interactions are sticky, and you feel good in the moment because you are connecting with the person who is complaining, but negativity breeds negativity.

TOP TAKEAWAYS

Setting big goals starts with a plan. Being specific about your business development goals is key. Your personal objectives might include growth in the numbers related to your law practice—sales of legal services, billable hours, and increased profitability generally for your firm. Your business development objectives might relate to developing a new practice area for your firm or even a flat fee option for people looking for different price points. Be as specific as you can with the big goals. You will be working on them weekly and even daily in some situations, so you will want to visualize what success looks like so you can write it down and track it.

Smaller tasks that support the health and viability of your long-term goals are the power behind your plan. Attorneys who are focused on business development and personal branding know in advance what the tasks are for that week and what the goals are. Some people take 30 minutes on Sundays to plan out their business development for the week; others use software to help them manage their responsibilities. Whatever your system is, use it, regularly. These micro-tasks will turn into habits, as you will know on Mondays, when you check your LinkedIn. On Wednesdays, you post on LinkedIn; on Fridays, you like/share/comment on your colleagues' LinkedIn profiles. This general idea of what your week looks like paired with activities that you can afford to do—moneywise and timewise—will keep your progress moving.

Writing down your tasks or adding them to task-management software is helpful in making these intangible ideas into real activities you need to do and take care of. You should take your business development operations as seriously as you take your other operations. This can be through commitment to an operational plan of how things will work or even a checklist that you update every week by adding new items or checking off what has been completed. Having a tactical plan increases your progress. You don't start out on top; you earn your way there through consistent activities that support your bigger brand and your goals.

This consistency in your actions is key to hitting your business development goals. Committing to taking deliberate actions daily, weekly, and monthly that align with your overarching goals isn't enough. Clarifying how you will measure your strategy and its progress is imperative to consistent advancement. Business development in a small law firm environment or solo practice can feel lonely. It might feel weird to share with your friends that you just met a great connection and why that matters for your long-term business development strategy. It's just not something many people talk about or know how to react to when you talk about it. But talk about it anyway. Be proud of your successes.

You need to find ways to celebrate your wins because no one else will do it for you. You will want to build in time to look back and reflect on how far you have come—because you are the only one who will know how hard that mountain was to climb. Everyone will just see you at the top. It is true that sharing your success can be tricky. While you might want to give shout-outs on your LinkedIn page to yourself for securing new clients, that might not be the classy or ethical thing to do. Rather, you can share your success by writing a case study for your website, sending a thank you note to a new client for engaging your firm, or rewarding yourself with an awesome dinner. Celebrating big and small wins is important in business development, and your colleagues at your firm, your family, and your friends should welcome hearing great news when you have exciting developments. This is especially true when you are around people who are focused on growth and goals like you are.

Conclusion

Achieving anything significant takes time and energy. Each chapter in this book builds you up as a professional and strengthens your business development acumen. Holistic business development is a must for solo practitioners and small law firms. When it comes to accessing the type of professional development that leads to success, you necessarily have to plan for it all—the good, the bad, and the ugly.

But staying connected to your foundational vision for your career is what will transform it. The *why* behind everything you are doing is what will keep you going when the couch is calling, or you just don't feel like attending that board meeting this week. Your brand will reflect the *why* and help you create a mission that reflects your value and values. Be sure to say yes a few times outside your comfort zone or box, and remember that having collegial relationships and having fun are big parts of keeping you engaged in the work that comes with long-term business development for your solo or small law firm. So, even if you only have an extra hour a day or every other day to commit to your business development, use this time intentionally and wisely.

Relationships can be started with a smile, and connections are made in the moments.

Glossary

This glossary is intended to provide a further explanation of key marketing and business development terms as they are used in this book and how they relate to the legal industry.

Term	Definition
B2B	Business-to-business, or B2B, is the business model that applies to lawyers who sell their professional services to other businesses. These types of client engagements are usually complex, with repeating and long-term engagement with the law firm.
B2C	Business-to-consumer, or B2C, law practices follow a business model that offers their legal services directly to consumers. As these types of legal engagements are shorter in engagement, B2C law firms have to strategize and market to account for needed volume and expected turnover.
Business Development Strategy	A business development strategy is a broad plan that provides definition, shape, and direction to a law firm as a business or to a lawyer in their legal career. It is distinct from the tactical strategy, which outlines the steps needed to execute it. The business strategy answers questions such as "What are my business goals?" and "Why are they my business goals?" In contrast, a tactical strategy addresses the practical steps needed to execute the plan and answers very different questions, such as "How will I achieve my business goals?" and "What do I need to do today, tomorrow, and next month?"
Career Sponsorship	Career sponsorship is a relationship wherein the more senior lawyer utilizes their leverage and influence to create opportunities for their career. Career sponsorship goes beyond the advice and guidance of career mentorship to advance others through actions and activities.

Term	Definition
Collateral Materials	"Collateral materials" is a collective term used to describe the media needed to sell legal services. Typical printed collateral materials include law firm business cards, flyers, one-sheets, and brochures. Collateral materials are also digital. Typical forms of digital collateral materials include online ebooks, magazines, and videos. Collateral materials include law firm "swag," branded items for giving away, such as pens, water bottles, and stickers with your law firm logo.
CRM	A CRM software tool helps you manage and store information regarding your business relationships with clients and referral sources. A CRM can improve your sales cycle by tracking your interactions throughout the year and providing reminders to check in regularly with people in your network. A CRM captures your network data, including your business contacts' names and email addresses, keeping it organized and accessible. There are tons of digital software options for CRM systems for small law firms, with most integrating with email systems such as Outlook.
DEI	Diversity, equity, and inclusion, or DEI, are related to increasing inclusivity, value, and respect for diverse populations. Inserting DEI into business development helps widen the lens of the law firm and can lead to a stronger reputation, a wider pool of potential clients, and increased empathy in a law practice.
Demographics	Demographics are statistical data about a population or market, including information about family size, income, location, and language. Law firms utilize demographic data to create market segments for specific legal services, products, or marketing campaigns. Understanding these demographics helps firms make more targeted and measurable marketing and business development decisions. Audience demographic data can be researched online through various U.S. government websites. Additionally, demographic information can be obtained from the business insights of social media platforms like Facebook and Instagram.
Elevator Pitch	Elevator pitches are concise 30-second statements of about 75 words, about how you help through your legal services.

Term	Definition
Email Campaigns	Email campaigns are a series of emails that your law firm sends out. These emails relate to your legal services and can include updates about your law firm and attorneys, including awards, publications, and new memberships. Email campaigns can advise on changes in the law through alert notifications or links to thought leadership published on your blog. For small law firms, email campaigns are a great way to build rapport with an audience through visibility and consistency. They are also a low-cost way to drive traffic to your website and market your legal services. Email campaigns are set up deliberately using online tools such as MailChimp and Constant Contact.
Evergreen Content	Evergreen content is a widely used marketing term. This type of content doesn't expire or stale, so it is "evergreen" like coniferous trees. Evergreen content for law firms can look like answers to frequently asked questions and case studies. This content is always interesting or always applies to the audience. It can answer common questions or provide general educational value. Law firms use evergreen content to send to potential clients, and they use it in their marketing materials. Because this content doesn't require consistent updating, it is a reliable marketing option for the firm to use in business development.
Firmographics	Firmographics are data used to categorize businesses in a way that enhances an understanding of their characteristics. This data can include factors such as industry, revenue, and financial performance, which help law firms identify which businesses might benefit most from their legal services. Firmographics are found through public records searches, as well as in paid legal industry databases. Social media platforms, particularly LinkedIn, also aggregate this information for millions of companies, making it an accessible resource for smaller law firms. By leveraging firmographics, law firms can make informed business decisions regarding their target audience, messaging, pricing, and services.
Geotargeting	Geotargeting is location-based digital marketing. Geotargeting uses IP addresses, GPS, and cellular data to deliver targeted content to specific audiences. It can be used through business pages on social media platforms, including Facebook and LinkedIn. It is also available through advertising on major search engines such as Google and YouTube. Geotargeting comes in a variety of formats, including push notifications sent to phones through geoadvertising.

Term	Definition
KPI	Key performance indicators, or KPIs, are metrics that bring business development goals to life. They quantify efforts related to business development and marketing success through trackable data. KPIs help law firms make their business development efforts quantifiable.
Marketing Funnel	The marketing funnel for a law firm is the purchase cycle that tracks how they meet potential clients through signed engagement letters and loyalty. A marketing funnel is the deliberate mapping of how you intend to convert potential clients from complete strangers to your law firm to signed engagements. A small law firm's marketing funnel is necessarily part of its business development strategy. For example, suppose a small law firm would like more visibility in the legal community. In that case, they may include bar association events participation in their business development strategy and accompany that effort with their marketing funnel. Their marketing funnel could include a monthly email campaign to stay in contact with the lawyers they meet at the bar association events.
Micro-Credentialing	Micro-credentialing in business development relates to learning specific skills or seeking out education in a unique area of knowledge. Micro-credentials don't have to be full-blown degree programs, but they can be. Micro-credentials increase expertise in a particular area and can further be displayed on your CV and website to validate your qualifications to potential clients and referral sources. Attorneys can find short programs, online certifications, and the like to give them more competency in a particular area. For example, an intellectual property attorney could pursue micro-credentialing in an area of AI that they intend to seek clients. Or a DUI attorney might want to know more about breathalyzer calibration for use in their defense cases.
Niche	A niche is a focused law practice. Niche law practices serve a specific audience within a larger market with services that apply to a particular demographic or legal need.

Term	Definition
Personal Brand	A personal brand for a lawyer is a powerful means to define their identity. It communicates who they are, what they do, and the value they bring to their community. In a solo law firm setting, a personal brand communicates the lawyer's practice area strengths and the unique value they bring to the community. In a small law firm setting, the personal brand of the attorneys should be distinct from the law firm's brand as a business. The personal brand of the lawyers in a small law firm should complement each other and the law firm as a business but also be unique to the lawyers as an expression of their individuality, strengths, and the value they add to the community.
Time Blocking	Time blocking is a time management technique that encourages you to schedule dedicated blocks of time for specific activities or tasks. It helps you focus on one task at a time, minimizing distractions and boosting productivity.
Value Proposition	A value proposition is a statement that informs potential clients or referral sources about your legal services. It succinctly shares why your law firm is a good choice for specific legal issues or the clear, measurable benefits of working with your law firm.

About the Author

Meranda M. Vieyra owns Denver Legal Marketing LLC. She is one of the most visible legal professionals in the West, with 20+ years of experience in the legal industry. Her award-winning marketing techniques and business acumen have earned her a strong reputation as the go-to for impactful legal marketing and business development strategies and have significantly transformed the marketing landscape for lawyers and law firms.

Meranda's visionary creativity has led to many accolades and a well-credentialed career. In addition to being a business owner, she is a lecturer and author on marketing and business development. She served as an adjunct professor at her alma mater, MSU Denver, in 2020. In this capacity, she created and taught the first class in the country on legal marketing at the undergraduate level. She was honored to be named to the 40 Under 40 list by the Denver Business Journal (2018) and given the 10 Under 10 Award by the Metropolitan State University of Denver Alumni Association (top ten alum of the decade). In 2019, Meranda was named one of the Top 25 Most Powerful Women in Business by the Colorado Women's Chamber of Commerce and one of the Top 100 Young Professionals in Colorado through the Gen XYZ Awards published by ColoradoBiz Magazine. The National Law Review named her a "Go-To ThoughtLeader" in 2020 and she was one of the recipients of the esteemed Denver Business Journal's Outstanding Women in Business in 2021. Meranda was honored to receive the Inclusiveness @Work Business Corporation Award from the Center for Legal Inclusiveness in 2022.

Meranda lives in Colorado with her husband and two daughters. She is a devoted yoga practitioner, an adventure traveler, and a lifelong student of Mesoamerican history.

www.DenverLegalMarketing.com

Acknowledgments

No one does it alone. I have so many people to thank who have helped me throughout my career and led me to this book-writing journey. But here's a few who come to mind.

My husband, Gordon Nichols, whom I walk proudly beside as his wife. You bring resilient support, love, laughter, and honesty to my days. You are my fiercest advocate and most crucial ally in life and business. We have done this together.

My stepfather, Mitch Geller, knew I was scrappy and smart enough to work for his solo practice law firm. I was an 18-year-old college student who had just moved out of his house. At the time, I needed a job, but I now realize that I actually got a chance. You opened the door to my legal career.

My book liaison, John Mitchell with the American Bar Association, for the opportunity to share my knowledge more widely than I ever imagined. Your choice to champion my voice and perspective on small law firm business development made my dream of "maybe one day" writing a book a reality.

My colleagues in the legal community, for many years of friendship and fellowship as we navigated the craziness of legal industry work. Some of us met as far back as 1998 as co-workers in law firms, and we grew up together. Others came into my world as clients when they trusted me to work with their law firms. Regardless of how we met, know that I have laughed with you as much as I have learned from you.

